Contents

Jacket: A painting by Repin of the
crowd being shot down on 'Bloody Sunday',
22nd January 1905
Front endpaper: Strikers in the streets
of Kharkov, July 1905
Rear endpaper: Russian dead during the
Russo-Japanese war

Copyright © 1969: David Floyd
First published 1969 by
Macdonald & Co (Publishers) Ltd
St Giles House 49 Poland St London W1
in the British Commonwealth and
American Heritage Press
551 Fifth Avenue New York NY 10017
in the United States of America
Library of Congress Catalogue Card
Number: 72-83791
Made and printed in Great Britain by
Purnell & Sons Ltd Paulton Somerset

RUSSIA IN REVOLT

1905: The First Crack in Tsarist Power

David Floyd

Macdonald Library of the 20th Century
General Editor: John Roberts

Chapter 1
The Tsar and Tsarism

Within three months of his becoming Emperor of Russia in October 1894 Tsar Nicholas II received delegates from many of the main Russian cities and towns. They came to him with loyal addresses, welcoming the accession of the young Tsar to the throne and assuring him of their loyalty, but also expressing some timidly worded hopes that the ordinary people of Russia might, through their representatives, have some say in the government of the country. Nicholas's reply to the delegates was curt and uncompromising. He was glad, he said, to hear their 'sentiments of loyal allegiance'.

'But' — he added — 'it has come to my knowledge that voices have been heard of late in some *zemstvo* [local] assemblies of persons carried away by senseless dreams about their representatives participating in the administration of the internal affairs of the state. . . .

'Let every man know that, while devoting all my strength to the well-being of my people, I shall uphold the principle of autocracy as firmly and as undeviatingly as did my late father.'

His father, Alexander III, had done much in the course of his brief reign to undo the good which *his* father, Alexander II, the 'Tsar-Liberator', had done in the period of the 'Great Reforms'. On his ascent to the throne in 1881 Alexander III had affirmed his faith in autocratic rule in these words:

'In the midst of our great grief God's voice commands us to stand courageously at the helm of the government, relying on Divine Providence, with faith in the power and truth of the autocracy which, for the benefit of the people, we are called upon to strengthen and protect from any encroachments.'

Alexander's absolute faith in the virtues of autocracy and his God-given duty to preserve the unlimited power of the Russian monarchy intact and hand it on unchanged to his successor was encouraged by the man who had been first his tutor and later became his principal adviser

Left: The coronation procession of Tsar Nicholas II passes through the crowded streets of Moscow on 26th January 1896

on affairs of state – Konstantin Pobedonostsev. This intellectually brilliant but bigoted and misanthropic character exerted the most powerful influence over Alexander throughout his reign and over his son, Nicholas, at least during the first decade of his rule. He had a semi-religious faith in Russia's destiny coupled with utter contempt for the West, its ideas, and its institutions.

'The day may come,' Pobedonostsev told Alexander, 'when flatterers will try to persuade you that, if only Russia were to be granted a "constitution" on the Western model, all problems would vanish and the government could carry on in peace. This is a lie, and God forbid that a true Russian shall see the day when it becomes an accomplished fact.'

In 1901 he was still telling Nicholas that a constitution would be 'the ruin of Russia'. It was 'the fundamental evil', and parliamentary government was 'the great falsehood of our time'. Such were the views instilled into Nicholas from early childhood and which he retained unaltered until he and the autocratic system he so obstinately defended collapsed in 1917.

But where his father had been strong and decisive Nicholas was relatively weak and easily influenced. 'The Emperor's character may be said to be essentially feminine,' said Count Sergei Witte, his Minister of Finance. 'At first any official coming in personal contact with him would stand high in his eyes. His Majesty would go beyond the limits of moderation in showering favours on his servant, especially if it were someone appointed by him personally and not by his father. Before long, however, His Majesty would become indifferent to his favourite and finally turn against him. His Majesty would not tolerate about his person anyone he considered more intelligent than himself or anybody with opinions differing from those of his advisers.'

Witte, never a kindly critic of the Tsar, summed up Nicholas's view of his role thus: 'I do what I please, and what I please to do is good. If people do not understand it, that is because they are ordinary mortals, while I am God's anointed.'

Despite his belief in the destiny of the Russian people and his duties as their sovereign, Nicholas remained throughout his life remote from the ordinary people. Nothing could have demonstrated this remoteness **11** ▷

Right: The Tsar regarded himself as God's anointed; to his people he was the 'Little Father', their absolute ruler who must be obeyed without question. These attitudes naturally meant that the Church with its elaborate ceremonies and processions was one of the strongest pillars of the Tsarist state
Next page: The inheritance of Nicholas II. The coronation of Alexander III in 1881 typifies the Tsarist ideal of unlimited power

more clearly than the disaster which accompanied his coronation in Moscow in 1896. Mismanagement by the police resulted in a stampede by the crowd of some hundreds of thousands who had gathered on the Khodynka field. Nearly two thousand people died that afternoon. But it did not affect the Tsar's plans for the day.

'A gorgeous evening party was scheduled for the same day, to be given by the French Ambassador, the Marquis de Montebello,' Count Witte recalled. 'We expected the party to be called off because of the Khodynka disaster. But it took place, as if nothing had happened, and the ball was opened by Their Majesties.'

Nicholas kept himself remote, not only from the common people, but also from the upper classes and even from his own courtiers. He had no friends or intimates, and even his closest advisers could never know when they might find themselves dismissed. Even the grand-dukes—the members of his own family, mostly cousins and uncles—many of whom held high positions in the administration, had access to the Tsar only two or three times a year. Only three of his uncles were given the right to offer him advice, without, however, having any assurance that he would take it.

It was a direct result of this remoteness that the person who, in the latter part of his reign, exercized the greatest influence over Nicholas was his wife, the Empress, or Tsarina, Alexandra Fyodorovna. 'Alix', as she was known to the Tsar and her closest friends, was born Princess Alice of Hesse-Darmstadt, the daughter of Princess Alice of England. Educated by her grandmother, Queen Victoria, at Kensington Palace in London, she married Nicholas in 1894, the same year as he ascended the throne, and they remained devoted to each other until the day in 1918 when they were murdered by the Bolsheviks. But Alix was even more retiring than her husband, and this, combined with her weak health and her extreme devotion to the Orthodox religion, to which she had of necessity become a convert, served only to confirm the Tsar in the rightness of his ways. She was if anything even more blindly determined to defend the autocracy than was the Tsar himself, and whenever he was inclined to make any concession to liberal pressures, a word from Alix was usually sufficient to stop this.

The situation became even more sinister when, in 1905, Alix herself fell under the baleful influence of Grigori Rasputin, the 'man of God' who won the confidence of the Empress in the first place by persuading her that he could stop the bleeding of Alexei, the long-awaited heir

Left: The State Council in session. This body consisted of elder statesmen who had little influence over the actions of the Tsar

to the throne, who was afflicted with haemophilia. Rasputin was a *starets*, or wandering preacher, who had managed to work his way into St Petersburg society. He was a peasant by birth, and illiterate at that, and his teaching, a mixture of eroticism and mysticism, appears to have been that sexual indulgence is the key to humility and hence to eternal salvation. His influence with the Empress, and through her with the Emperor himself, reached such proportions that he was able eventually to secure the appointment and dismissal of ministers. The scandals which surrounded him did much to discredit the monarchy and Nicholas's authority in the public eye.

The part played by Rasputin in the Tsar's councils was the *reductio ad absurdum* of autocracy, or dictatorship. With all power concentrated in the hands of one man, that power turned out to be at the disposal of the first charlatan who succeeded in worming his way into the dictator's confidence.

Though Nicholas was determined to keep all decision-making in his own hands, he could not, of course, govern Russia without help in the form of administrators and even advisers. Nicholas's empire covered 8,500,000 square miles, and stretched from the Baltic and the Carpathians to the Pacific and the borders of China and India, and from the Arctic to the Black Sea. Much of it consisted of empty wastes, but still the population had reached more than 130,000,000 by the end of the 19th century. Not only was the population spread out thinly over a vast area; it was a patchwork of races, languages and cultures. Only 55,000,000 of the population of the Russian empire were 'Great Russians' speaking Russian as their mother tongue. The rest were either related Slav peoples – Ukrainians, Belorussians, or Poles, totalling 36,000,000 – or Baltic peoples (4,000,000), Caucasians (3,500,000), Kazakhs, Uzbeks, or Turkmen from Central Asia (7,000,000), Tartars (4,000,000), Germans (2,000,000), Jews (5,000,000), and Mongols or members of nomadic tribes in the Far East and North. The task of ruling and controlling such a vast and variegated population, the majority of whom were illiterate and engaged in primitive agriculture, was not easy. Witte himself is said to have commented:

'The outside world should not be surprised that we have an imperfect government, but that we have any government at all. With many nationalities, many languages, and a nation largely illiterate, the marvel is that the country can be held together even by autocratic means.' The problem was not simply one of size and complexity; it involved intense national feelings. The non-Russian peoples were for the most part unwilling citizens of the Russian empire, and nationalism added fuel to the fires

of political and economic discontent. The official policy of St Petersburg towards Poland, Finland, the Baltic provinces, the Ukraine and the Caucasus in the final decades of the 19th century was one of outright 'Russification', which aimed at nothing less than the complete elimination of the native languages and cultures of those areas. Thus, people of Polish origin and Roman Catholic faith were excluded from all official positions in Poland, and the use of the Polish language in primary and secondary schools was forbidden. The Russian language and Russian officials were similarly imposed on Finland towards the end of the 19th century. Such measures served only to increase opposition to the Tsar's rule and to convince the non-Russian peoples that the downfall of Tsarism was the essential prerequisite to a solution of their own political and social problems. The nationalist movements which grew up around the periphery of the Empire alarmed the authorities in Petersburg and prompted them to exploit Russian chauvinism in reply.

The framework of the empire
It was this preoccupation with the problem of holding the empire together that determined the shape and nature of the Tsarist administration. It was a highly centralized, bureaucratic hierarchy of officials, whose main function was to enforce laws and decisions drawn up in the imperial capital. Their job was primarily to transmit power outwards from the centre.

Most important were the governors-general and governors of the ninety-six provinces into which the Russian Empire was divided at the beginning of this century. A governor-general was both the civil and the military head of a group of provinces, usually of those with a non-Russian population. A governor was in charge of a single province, and in addition there were four 'prefects', each responsible for one of the four cities of St Petersburg, Odessa, Sevastopol, and Kerch. The power of these officials, appointed by the Tsar and answerable only to him, was practically unlimited. Any limitations there were on their authority could be removed if the Tsar, acting in accordance with the 'Exceptional Measures' Law of 1881, chose to place a province or city under 'reinforced protection' or 'extraordinary protection'. More than half the territory of the Russian empire, including most of the major cities, was under one form of 'protection' or other by 1904. Any form of public protest or political opposition to the régime, real or imagined, was sufficient justification for the Law to be invoked.

Left: Moscow, the spiritual centre but not capital of Russia

The government department responsible for the administration of the empire's internal affairs was the Ministry of the Interior, which also controlled all the various police organizations whose main task was to smell out, pursue, and punish all critics and opponents of Tsarism. Apart from the customary police force, there were special city and rural police, factory police and railway police, and, of course, political police. The latter, organized as the 'Corps of Gendarmes', operated independently and arbitrarily, frequently without reference to the civil authority or the judiciary. In practice the police controlled every aspect of life in Russia, including movement about the country and the collection of taxes. The individual citizen could do little without first obtaining authority from the police, and that usually depended on the giving of a substantial bribe.

One of the most important functions of the Ministry of the Interior and its police organization was to enforce the censorship of all publications. Special rules laying down what could and could not be written or published in the press in Russia had been issued in 1865, and in 1882 additional 'temporary' regulations were imposed on the daily and periodical press. Editors who offended against the press rules were first warned and then, after three such warnings, obliged to submit their publications to the censor the day before they were due to appear. In addition, a committee consisting of the Ministers of the Interior, Justice, and Education, and the Chief Procurator of the Holy Synod had the power to suspend any periodical from appearing for as long as they chose and to debar editors from practising their profession. Towards the end of the century a great many editors and publishers were forced to give up this unequal battle with the authorities. It was in fact surprising how many of them managed to continue publication and to retain some independence despite the controls imposed on them.

'I believe that the government should not allow the control of the press to slip from its hands, and that it should not abandon this responsibility. To entrust it to the courts would be to give unbridled licence to the press, which would cause great harm to the state and the people.' To the end of his reign Nicholas acted in strict accordance with this precept, which Pobedonostsev delivered to Alexander III.

The ministers who headed the various departments of the administration were in a position similar to that of the provincial governors: they were appointed by **20** ▷

ANGELO·DELLA·PACE·I

The major tragedy of Tsardom

One of the most serious factors leading up to the storm which broke in 1905 was the nature of the man who ruled all Russia. A gentle family man **(top right** and **page 18)**, Nicholas II was totally unfitted to deal with the immense social and political problems which faced his country. From his father Alexander III he had inherited a grandiose belief in his absolute power, fittingly symbolized by this picture of the Tsar and Tsarina in medieval robes **(below),** and he was determined to cling to these powers against all opposition. In this he was encouraged and strengthened by his wife, Alexandra Fyodorovna **(page 19)**. The position became more sinister in 1905, and the great prestige which the Tsar still enjoyed among the common people was seriously damaged when the Tsarina fell under the influence of the illiterate and depraved Rasputin **(bottom right** with ladies of the court). Soon Rasputin's power was so great that he could make or break ministers and governments.

the Tsar to administer a particular department – finance, the railways, foreign affairs, education, and so forth – in accordance with his instructions. Like the governors of provinces, the ministers had considerable power within their own field of responsibility; but they had little influence, either individually or collectively, over the policy of the nation. When they met together as the Council of Ministers, it was only to discuss administrative questions and perhaps to tender advice to the Tsar, who always presided over their deliberations. He was under no obligation to take their advice, and the Council could not be regarded as a 'government' in the modern sense. It was often said at the time that Russia had 'ministries but no government'.

All ministers were members of another body which was also supposed to advise the Tsar on matters of legislation – the State Council. It was a sort of collection of elder statesmen, including many ex-ministers, governors-general and diplomats, whose main function was to submit bills to the Tsar for his approval. Again, the Tsar was in no way bound by the Council's recommendations, though he could not always completely ignore his most experienced advisers, some of whom had minds of their own.

The Tsar's critical minister

Of these the most distinguished was Count Sergei Witte, who served as Minister of Finance from 1892 to 1903, and then as Prime Minister from 1905 to 1906. Witte was a man of high intelligence and great administrative ability, hard-working and extremely ambitious. Like all those who rose to high office under the Tsar, he was a defender of the system of autocracy, but he did not allow this to blind him to the deficiencies of the Tsar himself. He was often at odds with Nicholas and his memoirs contain much spiteful criticism of the monarch and his wife. Of the class of nobility which surrounded the Tsar he wrote:

'I have, of course, never entertained any hostile feelings towards the nobility as a class. I am myself an hereditary nobleman and was brought up in genteel traditions. I am also aware that there are among our landed aristocracy many truly noble and unselfish men and women. All the great reforms of the sixties were carried through by a handful of noblemen, and today there are aristocrats who do not separate their welfare from that of the people and who sometimes serve the nation's cause at the risk of their own lives.

'But such noblemen are in the minority. The majority is politically a mass of degenerate humanity, which recognizes nothing but the gratification of its own selfish interests and lusts, and which seeks to obtain all manner

of privileges and benefits at the expense of the taxpayers in general, which means mainly the peasantry.'

Witte held the view, uncommon in Russia at the end of the 19th century, that the country's interests would be best served by the speediest possible expansion of its industry. 'A modern body politic cannot be great without a well-developed national industry,' he said, and he used his position as Minister of Finance to much good effect in extending Russia's railway network and developing her basic industries. He claimed to have increased Russian industry threefold during the decade he was minister.

'This again is held against me,' he commented. 'Fools! It is said that I took artificial measures to develop our industry. What a silly phrase! How else can one develop an industry? The measures taken by me were much less artificial than those practised by many foreign countries.'

In practice he maintained a protectionist tariff wall, stimulated the formation of joint-stock companies, issued industrial loans from the Imperial Bank and caused millions of men to be transferred from the land to industry and railway construction. He was the principal advocate of attracting foreign capital to Russia to assist his schemes. 'No country has ever developed without foreign capital,' he said.

Witte, with his own ideas about how the country should be run and his critical attitude towards the monarchy and the men around the Tsar, was not typical of Nicholas's senior advisers and administrators. Far more representative was Vyacheslav Pleve, who rose to the top of the police service in the reactionary reign of Alexander III and became Minister of the Interior under Nicholas in 1902. Though not a Russian himself, he was an ardent 'russifier' of the non-Russian peoples, a violent anti-Semite, and a willing executor of Nicholas's autocratic policies. A long feud between Witte and Pleve ended only when the latter was assassinated.

Despite the ruthlessness with which all signs of political opposition were suppressed, liberal and revolutionary critics of the Tsarist régime became increasingly active towards the end of the century. Important centres of liberal activity and thought were the *zemstva* — the elected councils in each province and county, first set up in 1864, which were responsible for certain local services and supplemented the organs of local government. Though it was limited to the purely Russian provinces and severely hampered in its activities by the local bureaucrats and police, the *zemstvo* was the beginning of self-government in the villages and encouraged hopes that it might be extended to the country as a whole. 27 ▷

Left: A street market in front of the Bolshoi Theatre, Moscow

The great obstacle to reform

Russia had always known great extremes of wealth and poverty. The upper class — the ruling nobility and great landowners — lived in considerable luxury (as is shown in the painting of a banquet on the **next page**), while the peasants in the poorer regions were often on the verge of starvation. These extremes persisted into the 20th century; but rapid industrialization in the latter half of the 19th century had created a new industrial middle-class. It was mainly from the ranks of the educated middle-class that the most important critics of the Tsarist régime came. But the would-be political reformers were too inexperienced, too lacking in self confidence, and too cut off from Western Europe to have a clear purpose. The gulf between the educated classes and the mass of the people remained vast — one of the main obstacles to political and social reform. The picture **(below)** typifies this gulf, while the *muzhiki* — wealthy peasants **(right)** — reflects the conditions of 19th-century Russia

Similar councils, called *dumas,* set up in the towns and cities did not have the same effect as the *zemstva,* because they became the preserve of the wealthy merchants and excluded the rising class of industrial workers. In practice neither they nor the poor peasants had any legitimate means of making their views known.

More radical political activity had of necessity to be carried on illegally, either as a conspiracy within the country, or directed from outside. The organization with the greatest following was the Social Revolutionary Party, whose members came to be known as 'SRs'. Though they rejected the teachings of Karl Marx, they stood for a form of socialism, adapted to Russian conditions and oriented towards the peasant. They were at the same time open advocates of terrorism and political assassination, which they regarded as the only means of forcing the Tsarist régime to grant concessions.

Meanwhile, towards the end of the century Marxist ideas began to spread throughout European Russia and the non-Russian provinces of the empire. Groups sprang up, mainly in the towns, among the workers and intellectuals, which came together in 1898 as the Russian Social-Democratic Labour Party. In 1903 the party split into Mensheviks and Bolsheviks, the latter being led by Vladimir Ulyanov, who came to be known as Lenin. The Marxists stood for the overthrow of the Tsarist régime by the people, led by a tightly organized and disciplined revolutionary party.

And so, at the beginning of the 20th century the Tsarist régime remained as rigid and autocratic as it had ever been, and under Nicholas's uninspired rule had even gone back on some of the reforms of Alexander II. But Russian society was not standing still; industry was growing rapidly, new towns were developing and a new class emerging. In towns and villages alike discontent was widespread, though largely mute.

Writing after the event, Trotsky's summary of the situation was:

'Nicholas II did not inherit from his ancestors just a vast empire; he inherited the revolution as well. They did not pass on to him a single quality to make him capable of governing the empire, or even a province or a district of it. To the progress of history, the waves of which were coming ever closer to the gates of the palace, unconcerned, the last Romanov turned a deaf ear: one might say that between his mentality and his age there had arisen a thin but utterly impenetrable wall.'

Left: Lenin (centre) with members of a revolutionary group in St Petersburg in 1897. In the following year several of these groups amalgamated to form the Social-Democratic Labour Party

Chapter 2
Economic change and stagnation

However much Nicholas II, his views, and his character may be held responsible for the disaster that overtook the Russian monarchy at the beginning of the 20th century, he cannot be held much to blame for the country's economic state. That was something he inherited from Russian history and his ancestors, and it can only be said that he was no more successful than they had been in their attempts to improve the economic condition of Russia and her peoples. By the turn of the century Russia was moving very fast into the industrial era; but the overwhelming majority of the population – more than 110,000,000 out of a total of about 130,000,000 – were still peasants, most of them scraping a miserable living from the soil. The existence of this enormous army of impoverished and largely illiterate peasants was Russia's greatest single economic problem, which continued to plague her rulers into the 20th century and which has, even today, still not found a satisfactory solution.

Alexander II had made a serious effort to grapple with the problem in 1861, by releasing the peasants from the state of serfdom in which they had been held for centuries. But his action did not come soon enough or go far enough to put Russia's rural economy on a sound footing. The main idea behind the 'emancipation' had been to create in the villages a class of small landowners who would, it was expected, become loyal supporters of the monarchy.

But the reform did not work out that way in practice. Instead of creating a large class of contented and prosperous farmers, it produced a relatively small class of fairly rich farmers and left the great majority of the peasantry as badly off as, if not worse off than, they had been as serfs. It was true that the Russian peasant had become in the eyes of the law a free man, but his economic lot was appreciably worse. He had been allowed to buy a plot of land only half the size of what he had cultivated before the reform and he had to pay for it by annual 're-demption' payments which were grossly overburdensome. The peasant farmer had no opportunity of making him-

Left: Rural Russia, market day in a typical provincial town

29

self economically independent, still less of improving his land and methods of cultivation. The most the majority of peasant households could hope to do was to grow enough for their own need, with perhaps a small surplus which could be marketed to pay taxes. The problem was further aggravated by the rapid growth of the rural population in the second half of the 19th century, when it nearly doubled itself, increasing from about 60,000,000 in 1850 to around 115,000,000 at the turn of the century. By then there were in some areas large numbers of 'landless' peasants who could not be usefully employed in the country and could not yet be absorbed into the towns.

The landowners also in trouble

It was not only the peasants and small farmers who found the going hard; the landowners themselves, many of whom had inherited large estates, also found it difficult to make farming pay, and so disposed of large areas of their land to the richer farmers or to the State. Nevertheless, the landlords as a class, of whom it is reckoned there were some 115,000, still owned in 1905 a total of 135,000,000 acres — about a third of the area owned by the 12,000,000 peasant households.

Hemmed in by the local authority, the landowners, and the tax collectors, the small farmer had no encouragement to improve his farming methods, even if he had had the means of doing so. He was cultivating the soil at the beginning of the 20th century in much the same, inefficient way as his forefathers had done before the 'emancipation'. Most of the ploughing was done by means of a wooden cultivator and not an iron plough; crops were harvested with the sickle or scythe and threshed with the hand flail. The strip system dominated agriculture, and this, added to the shortage of fertilizers, steadily drained the soils of even the richer parts of Russia of their goodness. A third of all the peasant holdings had no horse at all to help work the land, and another third had only one horse. The industry upon which Russia depended for the food to keep alive, and for providing the grain which was a valuable source of income, was utterly neglected and deprived of resources. From time to time the government, and even the Tsar himself, would appear to recognize the gravity of the situation and the danger which it represented to the national economy and political stability. Many special commissions were set up to examine the problem, but by the end of the century the situation was beyond responding to minor reforms, and those in authority could not bring themselves to introduce more radical measures.

The most remarkable feature of Russian agriculture in the 19th century, however, was that, despite all that has

been said above, it increased both its productivity and its total output. No less severe a critic of the Tsarist régime than Lenin himself produced figures to show that, in the forty-year period from 1864 to 1905 when the population of Russia increased by 75 per cent, the total grain harvest increased by 159 per cent and the potato harvest by four and a half times. Thus the amount of grain harvested per head of the population increased by nearly a half. At the end of the century there were more than 200,000,000 acres under grain in Russia, giving a total harvest of about four billion (4,000,000,000) poods, equal to about 65,000,000 tons. That was twice what it had been thirty years previously.

The landless or, in fact, unemployed peasant was not entirely without an escape from his dire situation. He could in some parts of the country hire himself out as an agricultural worker: there were between three and four million such workers towards the end of the century. Or he could seek to supplement or replace his income from the land by engaging in one of the many 'peasant industries', manufacturing a great variety of goods from furniture, baskets, and footwear to linen, carpets, and furs. These handicraft industries supplied many of the basic needs of the villages and also provided the basis for larger-scale production. At the beginning of this century more than 4,000,000 peasants were working full-time in these village industries, with another 8,000,000 giving part of their time to them.

Another solution for the impoverished peasant was for him to abandon his native village and migrate either to another region where the population was thinner and more land available, or to one of the rapidly growing industrial centres to become a factory worker. But, despite his 'emancipation', the peasant was not free to transfer his abode as he thought fit: he could migrate only with the express permission of his village commune and equipped with a proper internal passport. The authorities were not, however, interested in encouraging the drain of manpower away from the villages; they wanted rather to retain a plentiful supply of cheap labour. It was only towards the end of the century that, with some relaxation in the laws, the flow of migrants, mainly eastwards to Siberia, increased substantially. From about 10,000 in 1882 it increased to 108,000 in 1895 and more than 223,000 in 1899. Meanwhile the fact that in the final third of the century the urban population nearly doubled while the rural population increased only by a half was due to the influx of workers from the villages.

Left: *Village industry, landless peasants weaving baskets*

The result of the agrarian situation was that at the best of times, which meant in good harvest years, there were many millions of people in rural Russia on the fringe of hunger and with no security for the future. In bad years, when the harvest failed, as it did in 1891 and 1903, many millions were actually starving and millions more were undernourished. Often they went off roaming the countryside or raiding the towns in search of food. The dangers of such a situation were obvious, but no one seemed able to deal with it.

Trotsky defined the importance of the problem in the following terms:

'If the agrarian question, which had been inherited from the time of barbarism and Russia's age-long history, had been resolved by the bourgeoisie, if it *could* have been solved from that direction, the Russian proletariat would never have succeeded in taking power in 1917. For a Soviet state to be founded two quite different historical factors had to come together and interact: a peasant war — that is, a movement typical of the dawn of bourgeois development — and a working-class uprising — that is, a movement marking the decline of bourgeois society. Therein lies the key to everything in 1917.'

While Russian agriculture remained in the 19th century at much the same level, in terms of organization and equipment, as it had been in the 17th, Russian industry forged ahead at a relatively fast rate. Though it suffered the crises and recessions generally associated with a country entering the modern industrial age, by the beginning of the 20th century Russia already ranked as one of the world's great industrial powers.

Even at the beginning of the 19th century certain branches of Russian industry were well developed. This applied notably to the production of pig-iron in the Urals. But this was directed mainly to satisfying the country's military needs and was based largely on the use of serf labour. The emancipation of the serfs in 1861 undermined this type of industry and forced the industrialists to reorganize on the basis of a relatively free labour market. The old system was in any case hopelessly inefficient, as is revealed by the fact that, whereas Russia's output of pig-iron was roughly the same as Britain's in 1800, it was only a tenth of Britain's by the middle of the century.

Right: Diagrams which show the growth in Russia's urban and industrial populations and compare her industrial growth with that of Germany, the leading European power. Despite the apparent gap, Russian industrialization spread rapidly, and this is reflected in the fact that towns with populations of over 50,000 increased from thirteen in 1863 to forty-four in 1897

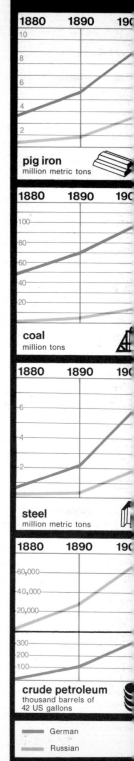

1880	1890	190

pig iron
million metric tons

coal
million tons

steel
million metric tons

crude petroleum
thousand barrels of
42 US gallons

German

Russian

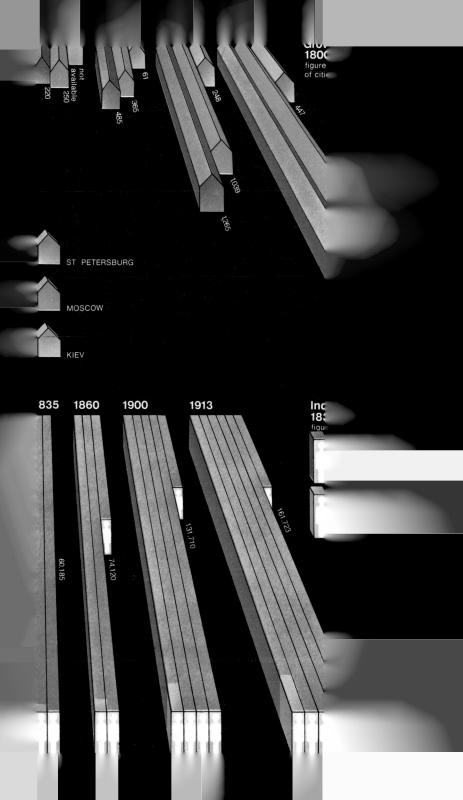

One of the main reasons for the rapid growth of Russia's industry at the end of the 19th and the beginning of the 20th centuries was the heavy participation in it of foreign capital, thanks in large part to Witte's efforts to attract foreign investors. Nearly 200 new foreign stock companies were set up in Russia in the last seven years of the 19th century, and the total amount of foreign capital invested in companies operating in Russia increased from 26,000,000 roubles in 1870 to 97,000,000 in 1880, 214,000,000 in 1890, and 215,000,000 in 1900. It was estimated that about a third of all corporation capital in Russia in 1890 was foreign; by the end of the century the proportion had risen to a half.

Prior to 1890 foreign investors were mainly interested in banking, insurance and railway construction. But there was a significant change in the last decade of the century when the investors shifted their attention to the manufacturing industries. Foreign capital accounted for 70 per cent of the total investments in the Russian mining industry in 1900 and was largely responsible for the fivefold increase in the industry's output in the last ten years of the century.

France and Belgium were the two countries most deeply involved in Russian industry, with Germany following close behind. Britain came fourth in the list, and the United States were nowhere in the running. A curious relic of this period survived until recently on the map of Russia. John Hughes, a Welshman, built a metallurgical plant in the Donets basin in 1869 and the settlement was called after him Yuzovka. Its name was later changed to Stalino.

Much of the increase in production was due, not only to the physical expansion of the industries concerned, but also to the introduction of better machinery, much of it imported from Western Europe, and the more efficient organization of the industrial processes. In particular the latter part of the century saw the concentration of basic industries in ever larger units—a process which, while raising the efficiency of production, and increasing output and profits, also brought the industrial workers together in large numbers where they could more easily discuss their common problems and grievances and arrange to bargain with the employers and the authorities.

There was no lack of cause for complaint. The influx of large numbers of workers from the countryside into the towns, which were badly equipped to house them and provide their needs, was a major social problem. Working conditions in the factories, which inherited some of the

Top left and *left: Scenes in Russia's growing industrial areas.*
Bottom left: Well-fed cabmen, traditional middle-class servants

traditions of the days of serf labour, were appalling. The workers never put in less than twelve, and more often were obliged to work sixteen or eighteen hours a day. In the absence of proper housing they often had to live and sleep in primitive barrack-like huts. There was a high proportion of female and juvenile labour. The ample supply of labour in the towns, which was being continually replenished by new arrivals from the villages, enabled the employers to keep wages low. They were reduced still further by the imposition of fines and other arbitrary deductions. Strike action was illegal and participation in strikes could result in a sentence of penal servitude. A factory inspectorate instituted in 1880 seldom interfered in conflicts between the employers and the workers.

The rapid industrial expansion of the end of the 19th century was followed by a serious economic crisis in the first years of this century. Factory owners began to cut down production, close factories, and dismiss their workers. The consequent unemployment and reduced wages aggravated the already strained relations between capital and labour and resulted in a nation-wide wave of strikes and industrial unrest, affecting almost every branch of the economy. In 1900 the miners in the Donets basin went on strike. In 1901 strikes were reported in St Petersburg, Moscow, Ivanovo-Voznesensk, Nizhny-Novgorod, Odessa, Tiflis, Saratov, Astrakhan, and in the Urals. The year 1903 saw a general strike throughout the southern industrial regions. These actions were for the most part spontaneous and primarily economic in character, but in some places they acquired a more general, political character with the intervention of the various revolutionary parties. In addition, the unrest spread to the peasants, who were also affected by the economic recession, and to the students, who themselves staged general strikes in 1901 and 1902. The country was seething with discontent and unrest, which often broke out into bloody conflicts between the protesting people and the armed police and military.

The authorities did not, however, seem to understand the strength of popular feeling or the explosive situation that was building up. They remained deaf to the demands of an army of working people who really had, in Marx's phrase, 'nothing to lose but their chains'. It was an army which, as Trotsky pointed out, amounted altogether, in the towns and the villages, to some 10,000,000 people – or with their families to 25,000,000 people – by 1905. It was a very large army to ignore.

Left: Cossacks keeping the peace at an oilfield. Strikes were a feature of Russian industrial life by the end of the 19th century, and troops sometimes had to be called out to restore order

37

Chapter 3
Disaster in the East

The troubles of the Russian monarchy in the early years of the 20th century were by no means all domestic ones. The same autocratic mode of rule which led to the build-up of tension at home also led Russia to disaster in her relations with the rest of the world. Nowhere was the lack of wisdom and sheer ineptitude of the Tsarist régime demonstrated more clearly than in the defeats suffered by the Russian armies and navy at the hands of the Japanese in the Far East. They were defeats brought about by the reckless pursuit of territorial expansion and material wealth.

Throughout the 19th century Russia played a substantial role in European politics and was recognized as a major European power. But by the end of the century any further extension of Russian influence into Europe seemed unlikely, and the Tsar and his advisers had to content themselves with the uneasy balance existing between the various powers. They therefore turned their attention to the Far East, to which they were attracted by the wealth and expanses of China and the absence, as they thought, of any other power capable of preventing them from realizing their political ambitions. As far as Nicholas was concerned the Japanese were 'monkeys', and it is doubtful whether he troubled to distinguish between them and the Chinese. He had no difficulty in finding advisers to support his plans. Prince Ukhtomsky developed the idea of Russia's 'mission in Asia', and Count Witte was an advocate of the 'peaceful penetration' of China which he thought would lead to Russia becoming the dominant naval power in the Pacific. An essential part of this plan was the construction of the Trans-Siberian railway, which was approaching completion at the end of the century.

China's defeat in the Sino-Japanese war of 1894-5 opened the way for an increase of Russian influence in China. Witte obtained for Russia an important role in China's finances and a concession to build the 43 ▷

Left: Russian infantry advance during the Russo-Japanese war
Next page: An optimistic Russian cartoon foresees victory

Chinese Eastern Railway across Manchuria, which was tantamount to Russian military occupation of the province. In 1898 the Russians were granted a twenty-five years' lease of the Liaotung peninsula and the right to build a railway from Harbin down through Mukden to Port Arthur (see map on page 50). By this time the other European powers, who were also not without their ambitions, were alarmed at Russian advances in the Far East and *de facto* occupation of Manchuria. But St Petersburg either ignored their protests or turned them aside with promises to withdraw, which they showed no intention of carrying out.

Once firmly established in Manchuria it was inevitable that the Tsar and his more nationalistic and adventurous advisers should turn their attention to Korea, which seemed ideally suited to further Russian ambitions in the Pacific. 'It is absolutely necessary that Russia should have a port open all the year round,' Nicholas had said in 1895 and indicated the Korean coast as the place for it. He was easily persuaded to give his approval to a scheme known as the 'Yalu River Concession' which was intended, under the guise of an enormous timber concession financed by Russian money in North Korea, to lead to the eventual annexation of the whole of Korea by Russia.

Korea was an area in which the Japanese considered they had a special interest, since it provided them with the most direct access to the Chinese mainland. They therefore tried to reach an understanding with the Russians for a division of spheres of interest. They were ready to recognize that Russia had some special rights in Manchuria, in exchange for a Russian acceptance of Japanese preponderance in Korea. But St Petersburg was not really interested in negotiations with the Japanese, whom they scorned. The Tsar took control of policy in the Far East completely out of the hands of the Foreign Ministry and put it in the hands of Bezobrazov, the man primarily responsible for the Yalu venture, and in 1903 he appointed one of Bezobrazov's associates, Admiral Alexeyev, to be his viceroy over the provinces of Kwantung, which included Port Arthur, and Amur.

At this the Japanese decided they had nothing to gain from continuing negotiations with the Tsar's government and they decided to act. At the beginning of February 1904 they broke off diplomatic relations with Russia, and on 8th February they launched a surprise attack with torpedo-boats on the Russian Far Eastern Fleet lying in Port Arthur. A second attack four days later left few of

*Top left: Another patriotic cartoon. **Bottom left:** General Kuropatkin, defeated at the Battle of Mukden. **Left:** The Russian army advancing during the mobile opening stages of the war*

43

the Russian ships undamaged and all of them locked in the heavily mined harbour. The Japanese had not bothered to make a formal declaration of war.

The Japanese attack took the Russian government completely by surprise; the Tsar and his advisers had long refused to take seriously the possibility of an attack by Japan. It was not surprising, therefore, that they were quite unprepared militarily to meet the attack. As the Japanese doubtless knew, Russia's own preparations for eventual military action in the Far East were far from complete. On the eve of the Japanese action General Kuropatkin, the Minister of War who was later to be given command of the Far Eastern campaign but who did not share the over-confidence of the Tsar's closest advisers, had said that Russia needed more than a year to be ready for a war.

The Japanese launch their attack

At the beginning of 1904 the Trans-Siberian railway, essential for the despatch of supplies to the Far Eastern theatre, was still incomplete for about 100 miles along the mountainous shores of Lake Baikal. Until it was finished supplies had to be ferried across the lake either by steamer or by light railway over the ice in winter.

Russian land forces in the Far East then amounted to about 100,000 regulars and 30,000 special railway troops spread out along the Chinese Eastern Railway. They were vastly outnumbered by the Japanese, who had started to mobilize as soon as they launched their attack and who, once the Russian fleet had been immobilized, were able quickly to reinforce their armies in Korea by sea. Neither had the Russian navy enjoyed a substantial superiority at sea, even before the attack on Port Arthur. Though the Russian fleet was slightly stronger in battleships, it was far less well-equipped with cruisers and torpedo-boats, and it had the use of only two widely distant naval bases — Port Arthur and Vladivostok. The Japanese had many home ports near at hand.

The Japanese also showed themselves to be in practice far superior to the Russians in the actual conduct of military and naval operations. This was perhaps not so much because the Japanese commanders were intrinsically better than their Russian counterparts as because they were less divided in their counsels. Kuropatkin and Alexeyev approached the campaign from entirely different points of view. Kuropatkin was for caution and for avoiding major engagements with the Japanese until Russian strength had been built up. Alexeyev shared the view current in St Petersburg that the Japanese were no match for the Russians in the field. The two men found it impossible to collaborate, but it was not until October

1904 that Nicholas at last reluctantly agreed to Alexeyev's withdrawal. 'I went through a painful inner struggle before I reached this decision,' he wrote.

A further weakness of the Russian position was the lack of international support for the Tsar's Far Eastern policies. The alliance with France was of little help, Germany was not ready to go very far in encouraging Russia as a counterweight to Japan, and Britain was openly the ally of Japan.

Despite all these manifest disadvantages, the mood in St Petersburg, encouraged by a section of the military and the press, was one of confidence. Witte records in his memoirs that, while Kuropatkin took the view that it would be sufficient if there were two Russian soldiers to every three Japanese on the Far Eastern front, a former war minister, Vannovsky, considered that one Russian to every two Japanese was enough to ensure victory. This sort of overconfidence in Russian arms and underestimation of the Japanese was to receive some very rude shocks in the course of the year from April 1904 to May 1905. The Russians were roundly defeated both on land and at sea.

The battles fought at sea were very brief but utterly disastrous for the Russian fleet and decisive for the outcome of the war. Without command of the sea the Russians could not prevent Japanese reinforcements reaching Korea or maintain their hold on Port Arthur. The Japanese plan was to immobilize the Russian fleet and bring the Russian armies to battle before reinforcements could arrive by land. Kuropatkin's general plan, which he was able to put into effect after Alexeyev's withdrawal, was, by retreating in good order, to avoid pitched battle with the Japanese until he had the resources to make victory possible.

At the end of February Admiral Makarov, one of the few really able Russian naval commanders, arrived to take over the Port Arthur squadron. But when he put to sea in his flagship, the *Petropavlovsk,* in the middle of April, he lost his life when the ship struck a mine and sank. This put the squadron out of action and exposed the base to bombardment by the Japanese. Then, in August, an attempt was made to bring the squadron out of Port Arthur to the safety of Vladivostok. It was intercepted and destroyed by Japanese ships under the command of Admiral Togo. A few Russian ships managed to take refuge in foreign ports, and five battleships, a cruiser, and three destroyers limped back into Port Arthur. They

Left: *Prisoners taken by the Japanese. The war proved to be a total disaster for the Russians. The troops were brave but ill-led by generals who failed to adapt their tactics to new conditions*

never attempted to sail forth again, remaining in the base as targets for the Japanese artillery.

Meanwhile things were going no better for the Russians on land. In April the Japanese forced their way quickly across to the Yalu river, where they engaged and defeated a Russian army superior in numbers and thus severed rail communications between Harbin and Port Arthur. They followed this in May by seizing Nanshan, which commanded the narrow neck of land north of Port Arthur. With the capture of the Russian-controlled port of Dalny (Dairen) the Japanese were in a position to besiege Port Arthur.

The Japanese began their campaign to take Port Arthur at the beginning of August 1904 with an assault lasting five days in which they lost 15,000 men. But the Russian garrison, under the undistinguished command of General Stössel, proved a very tough and expensive nut to crack. The siege was sustained for altogether 148 days, during which the Japanese lost a total of nearly 60,000 men — more than double the losses suffered by the Russians. By the end of December the garrison, reduced to about 20,000 men who still had some reserves of food and ammunition and were by no means desperate, was surrendered to the Japanese by Stössel. This left the Russian navy with only one usable base in the Far East — Vladivostok.

More Russian defeats and disasters

The rest of the war was fought out between enormous armies of Russians and Japanese in the mountainous, remote and climatically difficult terrain of Manchuria. In these battles the forces were more evenly balanced, with the Russians often outnumbering the Japanese. After the defeat on the Yalu in April Kuropatkin withdrew westwards towards the Mukden-Port Arthur railway line, on which, at Liaoyang, he was finally persuaded to give battle in August. There were 150,000 Russian troops against 135,000 Japanese. After a nine-day battle the Russians were obliged to withdraw further and finally dug in on the Sha-ho river twenty miles south of Mukden. There, at last, Russian reinforcements began to arrive by rail, and Kuropatkin found himself in September in command of 220,000 men against the 160,000-strong Japanese army facing him. Influenced by the knowledge of his numerical superiority and under constant pressure from St Petersburg to take aggressive action, 51 ▷

Top right: Wishful thinking before the disastrous battle of Tsushima. *Bottom right:* The end of Russia's fleet; ships sunk by the Japanese lie on the bottom of Port Arthur harbour. *Right:* Naval officers before the series of catastrophes began. *Next page:* Japanese troops triumphantly capture a Russian battery

Kuropatkin decided to go over to the offensive and 'force the Japanese to comply with our will'. But, despite the loss of more than 30,000 men and killing some 20,000 Japanese, the Russian commanders failed to make any serious impression on the Japanese lines. After such a battle the two armies, far from their supply bases and exhausted from their efforts, came to a halt and there was a lull for several months.

It was brought to an end by the surrender of Port Arthur, which released nearly 100,000 Japanese troops for fighting in Manchuria. By the middle of February the Japanese army before Mukden amounted to no less than 300,000 men, while the Russian forces had been raised to even more than this figure. The scene was set for what was to be, in terms of numbers of men involved, the greatest land battle in history. The result was a resounding, but not catastrophic, defeat for the Russians. Marshal Oyama carried out a brilliant encircling movement which forced Kuropatkin to withdraw from Mukden towards Harbin to the north. The Russians lost 90,000 men, the Japanese 70,000. But the Russian armies were not routed, and the Japanese were too exhausted to pursue them. The two armies remained facing each other south of Harbin until the end of the war, the outcome of which was finally decided, as it had begun, at sea.

In October 1904, before the surrender of Port Arthur, the Russian Baltic fleet set sail for the Pacific to achieve the victory at sea which was to turn the tide in the Far Eastern war. It was under the command of Admiral Rozhdestvensky. Even before the fleet had cleared the North Sea it was in trouble: as they passed the Dogger Bank some of the Russian ships opened fire on what they believed to be Japanese torpedo-boats and were in fact English fishing boats. This incident did nothing to endear British public opinion to the Russian cause.

In December Rozhdestvensky put into Madagascar, where he learned of the fall of Port Arthur, which resulted in no change of plan apart from the hasty despatch of some more antiquated vessels from the Baltic to join him. This whole fleet, consisting of eight battleships, twelve cruisers, and nine destroyers, finally reached the Far East in the spring. Heading northwards to Vladivostok, it entered the straits of Tsushima, between Korea and Japan, on 27th May. It ran straight into the fire of Admiral Togo's vastly more powerful and more efficient fleet and within a matter of hours the whole Russian squadron had been destroyed. Four of the battleships, seven of the cruisers, and five of the destroyers were

Left: *The empire of the Tsars, showing the main population centres west of the Urals and the single railway leading to the East*

sent to the bottom, four battleships and a destroyer were captured. Only one cruiser and two destroyers ever reached Vladivostok out of the twenty-nine vessels which had set sail from the Baltic. The Japanese lost only a few destroyers. Admiral Rozhdestvensky was taken prisoner and, after his eventual release, was court-martialled.

The extent of the Tsushima defeat was sufficient at last to cool the hottest heads in St Petersburg and even to make some of Russia's friends fearful lest Russia be eliminated altogether as a Far Eastern power. President Theodore Roosevelt brought the two warring powers together at Portsmouth, New Hampshire, in August 1905, and a peace treaty was signed after only three weeks' negotiations. The Russians recognized Japan's special interests in Korea and ceded to Japan the southern part of Sakhalin island, their control of the Liaotung peninsula, with Port Arthur and Dalny and the railway from Port Arthur to Changchun, 150 miles south of Harbin. Russia and Japan agreed to withdraw from Manchuria and return it to China.

The Treaty of Portsmouth marked the end, for the time being, of Russian expansion in the Far East. The actual losses in men and material suffered in the misguided war with Japan were of less importance than the additional damage the whole affair inflicted on the Tsar and his régime. It had suffered other blows at home in 1905.

Witte, who conducted the Portsmouth negotiations on behalf of the Russian government with considerable skill, summed up the results of the Russo-Japanese war in the following terms:

'In the early days of the Russo-Japanese war General Kuropatkin once reproached Pleve with having been the only minister to want the war and to side with the group of political adventurers who had dragged the country into it. Pleve retorted: "You are not familiar with Russia's internal situation. We need a little victorious war to stem the tide of revolution."

'History made a mockery of Pleve's calculations. Instead of enhancing the prestige and increasing the material resources of the régime, the war, with its endless misery and disgrace, completely sapped the system's vitality and laid bare its utter rottenness before the eyes of Russia and the world at large, so that the population, whose needs had been neglected for many years by a corrupt and inefficient government, finally lost patience and fell into a state of indescribable confusion.'

It is to this state of internal confusion that we now have to turn.

Right: Russian artillerymen. After Mukden the war reached stalemate with both armies dug in behind strong fortifications

Chapter 4
Bloody Sunday

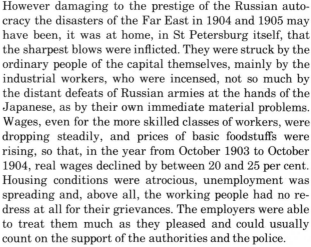

However damaging to the prestige of the Russian autocracy the disasters of the Far East in 1904 and 1905 may have been, it was at home, in St Petersburg itself, that the sharpest blows were inflicted. They were struck by the ordinary people of the capital themselves, mainly by the industrial workers, who were incensed, not so much by the distant defeats of Russian armies at the hands of the Japanese, as by their own immediate material problems. Wages, even for the more skilled classes of workers, were dropping steadily, and prices of basic foodstuffs were rising, so that, in the year from October 1903 to October 1904, real wages declined by between 20 and 25 per cent. Housing conditions were atrocious, unemployment was spreading and, above all, the working people had no redress at all for their grievances. The employers were able to treat them much as they pleased and could usually count on the support of the authorities and the police.

Georgi Gapon, a priest and former prison chaplain, wrote in his memoirs: 'I often watched these crowds of poorly dressed and emaciated men and women going home from the factories. It was a terrible sight. Their grey faces looked dead, with only their eyes, burning with the fire of desperate indignation, to enliven them. . . . After fifteen or twenty years of such a life both men and women often lose their ability to work and their jobs.'

Gapon himself was to play a leading part in the dramatic events of 1905. He was the leader of an organization of St Petersburg workers which had been set up with the approval of Pleve, the Minister of the Interior, and supported by funds provided by the secret police. He was in fact an instrument of what was known as 'police socialism' which involved the organization of unions for the working people, nominally to defend their interests and voice their grievances but actually to divert their revolutionary spirit and keep them under control.

At the end of 1904 relations between labour and management in the great 'Putilov' engineering works in **58** ▷

Left: Bloody Sunday, a photograph of troops firing on the crowd
Next page: An artist's dramatic impression of the same scene

the capital reached breaking-point. The employers' dismissal of some 'impudent' workers to 'teach them a lesson' brought the Putilov workers out on strike, and before long most of the main metal-working factories of St Petersburg were at a standstill. Gapon's 'Assembly of Russian Workingmen' became the central organization of the workers' protest, and Gapon himself came to be looked on as their leader, whether he wished it or not. It seems that this strange character was indeed swept along by the strength of the popular movement and that he sincerely believed that the Tsar would right the people's wrongs if only they could be brought directly to his attention. It was with this in mind that he conceived the idea of a workers' petition to the Tsar, to be presented to him publicly at the conclusion of a demonstration on Sunday 22nd January. Faith in the Tsar's fundamental goodwill towards his people was deep-seated in the Russian working people, and great hopes were placed in Gapon's action.

The plea of the workers

The petition was a remarkable document which, although in the event it did not produce the desired effect, reflects clearly both the spirit of protest and the naive faith in the Tsar prevailing at the time. It is doubtful whether it was purely Gapon's work; more likely it was a composite effort, embracing the demands, not of the working people alone, but also of groups of liberal intellectuals. It opened in a highly emotional tone:

Sire: We, working men and inhabitants of St Petersburg, our wives and our children and our helpless old parents, have come to You to seek truth, justice, and protection. We have been made beggars; we are oppressed and borne down by labour beyond our strength; we are humiliated; we are not treated as human beings but as slaves who must endure their bitter fate in silence. We have suffered this, and we are now being pushed ever further into the depths of poverty, injustice, and ignorance; we are being so stifled by despotism and arbitrary rule that we cannot breathe.

Sire: we have no more strength! Our endurance is at an end. We have reached that terrible moment when death would be better than the prolongation of our intolerable sufferings.

There followed a straightforward statement of what were manifestly workers' grievances and demands:

Therefore we have stopped work and told our masters that we shall not start again until they comply with our demands. We ask but little. We want only what is indispensable for life and without which there is nothing but toil and endless pain. Our first request was that our

employers should discuss our demands with us, but this they refused to do. . . . They regard as illegal our other demands: reduction of the working day to eight hours, the fixing of wage rates in consultation with us, investigation of our grievances against the factory managements, an increase in the daily rate for unskilled working men and women to one rouble, the abolition of overtime, medical attention to be given carefully and considerately, and the construction of factories in which it is possible to work without risk of death from wind, rain and snow.

Modest as some of these demands appear to us today, they constituted a very ambitious programme of reform in early 20th-century Russia. Implicit in the demands was the belief that the Tsar himself had no idea of how the 'capitalists' were treating their employees and that, once he did, he would take action to right the people's wrongs. But, in the words of the petition, those wrongs were not only economic: they were political as well. The 'bureaucrats' were just as bad as the capitalists:

Sire: there are many thousands of us here and, though we have the appearance of human beings, neither we nor the rest of the Russian people actually enjoy a single human right, not the right to speak, or to think, or to meet together to discuss our needs, or to take steps to improve our lot.

We have been enslaved, with the help and co-operation of Your officials. Anyone who dares to speak up in defence of the interests of the working class and the ordinary people is gaoled or exiled. . . . The whole people, both workers and peasants, are at the mercy of the bureaucratic administration, consisting of men who rob the government and the people. . . . Government by bureaucracy has brought the country to complete ruin, involved it in a shameful war, and is leading further towards disaster.

And so the appeal was for the Tsar himself to act:

This is why we have come to the walls of Your palace. Here we seek our last hope of salvation. Do not deny Your people help; lead them out of the depths of injustice, poverty, and ignorance; give them the possibility of controlling their own fate and being free of the yoke of bureaucracy. Tear down the wall between Yourself and Your people and let them rule together with You. . . . Examine our requests dispassionately and carefully: they are not evil in intent, but meant to help us and You.

So much a reasonable Tsar might have accepted; at least, he might not have been too offended. But then the petitioners went on to talk about constitutional government which was, had they known, anathema to Nicholas. Russia is too great [the petition continued] and its needs too varied and profuse to be governed by bureau-

Left: Father Gapon faces the Tsar's troops at the Narva Arch

59

crats alone. *Popular representation is essential. The people must help themselves and govern themselves. Do not refuse their help; accept it and order at once the calling together of representatives of the Russian land from all classes and sections of the people. Capitalists, workers, bureaucrats, priests, doctors, and teachers — let them all choose their own representatives. Let them all have a free and equal vote, and for this purpose order the election of a constituent assembly on the basis of universal, secret, and equal suffrage.*

Such demands went far beyond the rosiest dreams of the most liberal of reformers at the time, and certainly beyond anything the Tsar could have been expected to accept, even if he had been ready to receive the petitioners or listen to their complaints. The concluding words of the petition were no longer as humble as the opening. After presenting a list of specific demands, ranging from an immediate end to the war in the Far East to the proper control of overtime work in factories, the petition said: *These, Sire, are our main demands, about which we have come to You. . . . Order these measures and swear to carry them out. Thus you will make Russia happy and your name will be engraved in our hearts and in those of our descendants for ever.*

But if you do not give these orders or respond to our pleas, we shall die here in this square in front of Your palace. We have nowhere else to go and there is no point in our going. There are only two paths ahead for us: one leading to freedom and happiness, the other to the grave. Let our lives be a sacrifice for suffering Russia. We do not offer this sacrifice grudgingly but gladly.

This was the document which was to be presented to Nicholas on Sunday, 22nd January. However far-reaching its demands, there was no intention on the part of the organizers of the demonstration to cause trouble in the capital. Nor was there any secret about what they intended to do. The police and the Ministry of the Interior knew perfectly well what was being planned.

Count Kokovtsov, who was Minister of Finance at the time, recalls being summoned to the Minister of the Interior, Prince Sviatopolk-Mirsky, late on the eve of the demonstration. (Pleve had been killed by an assassin's bomb the previous July.)

'It was about nine or nine-thirty. In the minister's waiting room I met General Fullon, Governor-General of St Petersburg, Deputy Minister of the Interior General Trepov, and General Meshetich, Chief of Staff of troops in the Petersburg district. I had been summoned to hear reports from the generals on orders being given to

Left: Bloody Sunday, crowds begin to gather in Palace Square

61

military patrols in various parts of the city to prevent movement of workers from beyond the river and along the Schlüsselburg highway towards the Winter Palace.

'Here I learned for the first time that the priest, Gapon, was conducting an animated propaganda campaign among the workers and that he had had great success in inducing them to appeal directly to the Tsar. . . .

'There was no sign of apprehension or tension at the conference. When I asked why it met at such a late hour, Prince Mirsky replied that he had at first decided not to bother me at all, since the matter was not serious, especially since it had already been decided that the Tsar would not stay in the city on that day but would leave for Gatchina.'

According to Kokovtsov it was arranged that the police would let the workers know in good time of the Tsar's departure for his country residence so that the demonstration would be cancelled and 'there would be no gathering outside the Winter Palace'. 'No one at the conference considered it possible that the demonstration would have to be stopped by force, and certainly not that there would be bloodshed,' said Kokovtsov.

Witte, then President of the Committee of Ministers, later disclaimed any knowledge of what was afoot. He was not invited to the conference at Prince Mirsky's. But he was approached on the same evening by a group of 'public-spirited citizens', including the writer Maxim Gorky. 'The spokesman of the delegation begged me to see to it that the Emperor should appear before the workmen and receive their petition. Otherwise, they said, a great disaster was inevitable.'

There is, however, some evidence to suggest that, even if some ministers were kept in ignorance of the plans of the military and the police, the latter had made up their minds to use the demonstration as an excuse for teaching the rebellious workers a lesson. This was the view of Dr E.J.Dillon, correspondent of *The Daily Telegraph* in St Petersburg at the time. The Tsar was said to have made the Grand Duke Vladimir responsible for maintaining order. Of him a Russian author wrote: 'He will show no sign of weakness. He believes that the best way to cure the people of constitutional fancies would be to hang a hundred malcontents in the presence of their comrades. . . . Whatever happens he will tame the mutinous spirit of the crowd.'

The authorities certainly did nothing to dissuade Gapon or the workers from holding their demonstration, nor did they arrest the organizers. According to some reports, the military were put on to a war footing, ready to stop the demonstrators long before they could reach the Palace square. It was a reflection of the mood prevailing

in the country at the time that those in charge of the military and police were in a highly nervous condition.

'A pleasant Sunday outing'

For the demonstrators, on the other hand, the day was to provide a pleasant Sunday outing — as pleasant, at least, as the cold, grey wetness of St Petersburg in January would permit. While soldiers of the city's various Guards regiments assembled at key points and stamped their feet round their fires, the factory workers and their families began to gather at five or six assembly points in the city suburbs. The idea was that they should form up in columns and, setting off at different times, all arrive in the Palace square at about two o'clock in the afternoon. Gapon himself set out at the head of the column marching from the Narva hall; other clergy led the other columns, all of which carried ikons and pictures of the Tsar and Tsarina and sang hymns and patriotic songs. Such processions were a common sight in Russian cities in those days and the ones converging on the city centre that day evoked no especial attention from the people on the streets beyond the usual signs of respect for the religious banners and ikons. The police accompanied them along the route.

All went well with Gapon's column, numbering a few thousand people, until they reached the Narva Arch which celebrated Alexander I's victories over Napoleon. There the marchers found themselves confronted by armed police and troops and they were given the order to halt. They ignored the order and at once a detachment of horse guards galloped into them and broke them up. They hastily reformed and continued to move forwards. At this an officer ordered his troops to fire into the crowd, and after a few volleys the crowd turned and ran, Gapon among them. Twenty or thirty people were left dead or wounded on the spot.

The story with each of the other columns was much the same. In each case the sudden order to halt was followed almost at once by shooting and the shocked screams of the crowd as they ran from the bullets and the horses' hooves. As was inevitable with the military firing into an unarmed and unsuspecting crowd, the number of casualties was considerable.

But the shooting was not sufficient to turn the demonstrators from their original objective, the Palace square. On the contrary, it appears to have incensed the braver spirits among them and to have added to their number many sympathizers, students, and people who were simply curious to see what was happening. The result was

Left: Horse guards charge one of the columns of demonstrators

that many thousands of people, without organization or leaders (Gapon had gone into hiding), began to gather in the square in front of the Palace. Prince Vasilchikov, in command of the Guards, saw a danger of the crowd running amok, gave the order for the square to be cleared and then, when this proved ineffective, ordered his men to fire on the demonstrators. Once the square was cleared Vasilchikov ordered similar measures to be taken to disperse the crowds which had gathered at other points in the city, with the same effect. Hundreds of people were mown down.

One eye-witness account of some of the fighting comes from Count Witte himself: 'On the Sunday morning, I looked out from my balcony and saw a large crowd going along the Kamenoostrovsky Prospect. There were many intellectuals, women, and children among them. Less than ten minutes later shots rang out from the direction of the Troitsky bridge. One bullet whizzed past my head, another one killed the porter at the Alexander Lyceum. There was no one present to speak to the workmen and try to make them see reason. I do not know whether the same thing happened everywhere, but on the Troitsky bridge the troops fired rashly, without rhyme or reason. There were hundreds of casualties in killed and wounded, among them many innocent people. Gapon fled and the revolutionaries triumphed: the workmen were completely alienated from the Tsar and his government.'

There is no reliable record of what the total casualties amounted to. An official announcement admitted that about 130 had been killed and more than 300 wounded, but this concerned only those who were dealt with by the authorities. A group of journalists later produced a list of 4,600 people dead and wounded in the day's battles. The official figure is certainly low.

But far more important in the long run than the number of unfortunate people who were struck down by the agents of the Tsar on what came to be known in Russian history as 'Bloody Sunday' were the illusions about the Tsar and Tsardom which the police action destroyed. The autocracy had indeed, for the moment, reaffirmed its strength. But the sheer blind brutality with which the police and military acted did more than any amount of revolutionary propaganda to destroy the people's faith in their 'father'. For Lev Trotsky, the revolutionary leader, the events of that fateful day were all the proof that was needed that the working people of Russia's cities were an effective political force. 'The revolution has come!' he exclaimed. 'One move of hers has lifted the people over scores of steps, up which in time of peace we would have had to drag ourselves with hardship and fatigue.'

The Tsar remains unmoved

Not all Russian politicians saw Bloody Sunday in the same light as Trotsky, but most of them saw it as a disaster which would have far-reaching effects on the régime. Moreover, it did little to enhance Russia's reputation abroad. Count Kokovtsov recalls: 'The impression it created abroad was tremendous, and this just as I was negotiating for two independent loans, one in Paris and the other in Berlin.' The person on whom the whole affair seems to have had the least effect was Nicholas himself. When he came to make an entry in his diary for 22nd January, he could find no more to say than: 'A painful day! There have been serious disorders in Petersburg because workmen wanted to come up to the Winter Palace. Troops had to open fire in several places in the city; there were many killed and wounded. God, how painful and sad! Mama arrived from town; straight to Mass. I lunched with all the others. Went for a walk with Misha. Mama stayed overnight.'

Nevertheless Nicholas was persuaded by General Dmitri Trepov to do something which, following the tragedy of 22nd January, had the air of burlesque about it. Trepov had been made Governor-General of St Petersburg and had very much his own way in matters of public order, since Prince Sviatopolk-Mirsky soon retired from the scene and was replaced by Alexander Bulygin. Trepov proposed that, to appease the working people, Nicholas should summon representatives of the factories to his presence and personally assure them of his concern for their welfare. Nicholas was taken with this idea — 'provided sensible men were selected'. The 'sensible men' were selected by Trepov's men and the factory inspectors, and the whole affair was boycotted by the radicals in the factories. The 'delegates' were duly presented to the Tsar, who read them a little homily, sent them down to the kitchens for food and drink and packed them off home. One of them recalled: 'We returned to town by the ordinary train, and had to walk home from the station.'

This gesture by the Tsar had no effect at all on the temper of the people or to offset the impression created by Bloody Sunday. Kokovtsov was undoubtedly right when he commented that the rate of political developments would be determined rather 'by our military failures and the increase of public opposition, which was gradually becoming an open revolutionary movement'.

Indicative of the popular mood was the assassination soon after Bloody Sunday of the Grand-Duke Sergei Alexandrovich, Governor-General of Moscow.

Left: Father Gapon with the chief of the St Petersburg police

Chapter 5
Unrest and Opposition

The greater part of the year 1905 seems in retrospect to have been a period when the various political forces in the country – the autocracy, the more liberal-minded middle classes, the industrial workers, and the peasantry – were flexing their muscles and taking up positions for the more serious confrontation that was to take place in the autumn. It cannot be said that the Tsar and his advisers were unaware of the dangerous state the country was in or of the dangers which lay ahead. At the end of January Alexei Yermolov, Minister of Agriculture and a member of the Tsar's State Council, felt obliged to warn Nicholas of the threat to his rule:

'Although we succeeded by shedding blood on the streets of St Petersburg in bringing the workers' movement to a halt, this has not brought about any real pacification, rather the reverse. The agitation has not stopped, but may take on other forms, possibly finding expression in a number of attempted assassinations, which we believe the anarchists already to be preparing and against which nobody, not even yourself, Your Majesty, is secure, notwithstanding all the measures taken for your protection, and you must think what would happen to the State and the throne if an attempt were to succeed.'

Nicholas replied: 'I do not fear death, I believe in Divine Providence, but I know I have no right to risk my life.'

Yermolov's answer was: 'Yes, but you must think about the foundations on which your autocratic rule must rest. You cannot rely on armed force and troops alone. On 22nd January the soldiers certainly carried out the very difficult task which fell to their lot – to fire on a defenceless crowd. The unrest which started in Petersburg has now spread to most of the towns of Russia, and everywhere they have to be put down by force of arms.

'So far this is still proving possible and the soldiers are doing their duty. But, in the first place, what shall we do when disorder spreads from the towns to the villages, when the peasants rise up and when the slaughter starts

Left: By the autumn of 1905 tempers were running high as all classes joined in demanding far-reaching reforms from the Tsar

in the countryside? What forces and what soldiers shall we use then to put down a new peasant revolt, which will spread across the whole country? And, in the second place, Your Majesty, can we be sure that the troops who have now obeyed their officers and fired into the people, but who came from that very same people, and who even now are in constant contact with the population, who have heard the screams and curses hurled at them by their victims—can we be sure that they will behave in the same way if such incidents are repeated?'

Nicholas replied: 'I realize that the government's position is impossible if it has to depend only on the troops.'

The Tsar refuses all warnings

But Nicholas did nothing to change the situation, and Yermolov sent him an even more urgent appeal in the middle of February, this time pressing him to announce the holding of a nation-wide conference representing all classes of society. 'I know,' Yermolov said, 'that some people take the view that it would be dangerous to call representatives of the people together, especially in this troubled year when passions have been aroused, that demands might be made at such a meeting for a radical change in the ancient foundations of our state structure, for some limitation on the power of the Tsar, and for a constitution, that such a council might turn into a constituent assembly, that the peasants may raise the question of a repartition of the land, and that the unity of our Russian land might be threatened.'

Such dangers were less, in Yermolov's view, than what would follow if the existing troubles were allowed to spread. Then, he said, there would be no way of dealing with the situation—'and that will mean the end, not only of the Tsar's throne and of the autocracy, but of the whole Russian state.'

Yermolov was, as he said, a devoted servant of the monarchy, whose only thought was to save that institution. But he, like many others in the upper reaches of Russian society, as well as those already committed to programmes of liberal reforms, could see no way out unless the Tsar would grant the people or their representatives some say in the conduct of the country's affairs. Vaguely and reluctantly Nicholas recognized the strength of such arguments. But his own concept of his role as Emperor and the voices of many narrow-minded advisers in court circles, including his own wife, made it practically impossible for him to respond adequately or quickly enough to such words of wisdom.

The unrest foreseen by Yermolov spread rapidly through the towns of Russia and the outlying cities of

the Russian empire. Strike action by the industrial workers, in which political ideas often played as important a role as purely economic demands, spread alarmingly. Lenin pointed out that, while the average number of strikers each year during the decade preceding the year 1905 had been only about 43,000, the figure was more than ten times that amount in January 1905 alone and reached nearly 3,000,000 in the year as a whole. Lenin attached great importance to the 'mass political strike' as a means of educating and organizing the working people. 'The Russian revolution [of 1905] was' — Lenin said — 'at the same time a proletarian revolt, not only in that the proletariat was the leading force, the movement's *avant-garde,* but also in that the distinctly proletarian method of struggle, that is, the strike, was the principal means of swaying the masses and the most typical phenomenon in the formation of decisive events.'

The workers of the Putilov factory, who had been at the centre of the 22nd January demonstration, remained out on strike after the shooting. They were joined by other sections of the Petersburg population: the university students and most of the teaching staff refused to work and organized support for the strikers; lawyers, doctors, and members of other professions condemned the government's action and joined the call for a constituent assembly; the merchants of Petersburg refused to admit Guards officers to their club; even the manufacturers collected money for families of the victims; some 1,500 of the country's most distinguished scholars signed a demand for 'freely elected representatives of the people to have a say in government'; the press also took up the demand for the election of some form of national assembly. The strike movement spread first to Moscow, then to the Ukraine, Poland, the Baltic states, Finland, the Caucasus, and the dozens of Russian cities. For the most part these protests passed off without much violence or serious casualties, either because the authorities acted with sufficient force and firmness before trouble developed.

It was rather in the non-Russian areas, where nationalist emotions added fire to economic and political discontent, that the worst clashes occurred. A general strike in Riga, the capital of Latvia, led to a mass demonstration which was fired on by police and troops. Many who fled from the shooting were drowned as the ice on the Dvina river gave way. Most cities in Poland saw some violent clashes and the authorities there had to send for large reinforcements of troops.

This first wave of strikes did not, however, last long. It seemed more like a short, angry outburst of protest at

Left: Guardians of the régime, mounted St Petersburg police

the events of Bloody Sunday than the beginning of a more widespread movement. Short of money and food, and in the absence of any organization or leaders to keep up their spirits, the workers returned slowly to work. By the end of January they were all back in their factories, their lot largely unchanged.

It was not long, however, before the workers were out on strike again. The number of strikers was estimated at 80,000 in April, but rose to more than 200,000 in May. Much of this increase was due to the decision of the Socialists that May Day should be celebrated openly and accompanied by strike action. The appeal met with uneven response: in St Petersburg, where the people were presumably still intimidated by the events of Bloody Sunday, only a few hundred people turned out; but in some Baltic cities the strikes lasted several weeks and in other places there were serious clashes with the police.

One of the more important actions was the strike of 70,000 men and women operatives in the textile centre of Ivanovo-Voznesensk – Russia's Manchester or Pittsburg – 145 miles north-east of Moscow, which lasted ten weeks. To a long list of demands affecting their working conditions, including the eight-hour day, a minimum wage of twenty roubles a month, pensions, and the right to act collectively in defence of their working conditions, the strikers later added a demand for a constituent assembly. This was the first occasion, as far as is recorded, when the working people set up a *soviet,* or council, of delegates to represent them in dealings with the management. As the strike continued the *soviet* started to assume other functions of a political nature. This was the model of a form of 'direct democracy' which was to play an increasingly important role in the development of the revolutionary movement in Russia.

In the course of the spring and summer of 1905 the peasants were also drawn into the movement of revolt. Influenced by reports of unrest in the towns the peasants in some of the central Russian regions began seizing the estates, land, crops, and livestock of the landowners. Disorders of one kind and another were reported from 90 counties in the summer and had spread to 240 by the autumn. And, as Yermolov had forecast, this mood of revolt soon had its effect on the morale of the army, which was recruited almost entirely from the countryside. 1905 saw a series of mutinies among the soldiers in garrisons as far apart as Vladivostok, Tiflis, Tashkent, and Warsaw. They were a warning to the Tsar – which he seemed not to heed – that those troops on which he had relied so much to maintain his autocratic power might also be slipping over to the side of the revolutionaries.

The Battleship *Potemkin*

The act of mutiny which has subsequently been written into the legend of the revolutionary movement and given striking, if somewhat idealized, treatment in Sergei Eisenstein's classic film took place aboard the battleship *Potemkin*. (Its full name was *Prince Potemkin of Tauris*.) It was not in fact quite so glorious an event as it was later depicted.

There was a good deal of discontent in the Black Sea fleet in 1905, and revolutionaries of all kinds — Social-Democrats, SRs, and Anarchists — were all out to exploit it, and a plan emerged for a mutiny of the whole fleet at the time of the June manoeuvres. In the event only one ship mutinied — the *Potemkin*, the fleet's most recent and most modern acquisition. The mutiny started as a protest at the quality of the food served in the seamen's mess. When the admiral, in an act typical of the régime, ordered thirty of the protesting seamen to be shot, the firing squad refused to shoot, the potential victims rushed for their weapons, and the officers lost their heads and started to shoot wildly at the men. Within a very short time most of the officers had been thrown into the sea and the men found themselves, somewhat to their own embarrassment, in control of the ship, well stocked with food and fuel and ammunition.

Not quite sure what to do or where to go, the mutineers first put into Odessa, where they found a strike in progress. Unable to find anyone among the revolutionaries capable of taking command of the ship, the men appointed one of the surviving officers to carry out their instructions, and when the naval authorities sent practically the whole of the Black Sea fleet against the *Potemkin*, they sailed out and sent the fleet running. 'Fine goings on in the Black Sea fleet!' Nicholas wrote in his diary at this time. The *Potemkin* was joined briefly by the *St George*, which quickly surrendered, and soon afterwards the strike in Odessa collapsed. Since supplies were then beginning to give out, the crew of the *Potemkin* had no choice but to leave port, and they set sail for Constanta. At first the Rumanians refused to help, but when the *Potemkin* put in for a second time, the morale of her crew was very low indeed and they were allowed to surrender the ship and take refuge ashore. The mutiny was over.

It was scarcely a glorious victory for the mutineers, who were obviously quite unprepared for their brief success. But it was a very revealing and shameful episode for the Russian navy. The same incompetence that was producing disaster after disaster in the Far East was no

Left: Matsuchenko, leader of the mutineers (in the white shirt), shortly after the takeover of the Potemkin *on 27th June 1905*

71

less apparent in the peaceful waters of the Black Sea. It was hardly surprising that the Navy Minister decided to rename the *Potemkin* the *Panteleimon,* and so erase the memory of defeat at the hands of his own men.

While the mass of the ordinary people were giving vent to their feelings in strikes and mutinies the political opposition in the towns began to organize more purposefully. Here the lead was taken by liberal members of the professions, who formed themselves into 'unions' which joined together in June in the 'Union of Unions' which was presided over by the liberal leader Pavel Milyukov. Dominated by the left-wing liberals this body stood for the calling of a constituent assembly on the basis of universal, equal, direct, and secret suffrage. Later in the year the Union of Unions was joined by the newly-formed Peasants' Union, the first political organization ever set up to represent the Russian peasant.

Apart from the 'union movement and rather to the right of it politically was the *zemstvo* movement, which had succeeded in 1905 in setting up a central organization and linking up with representatives of the municipal *dumas*. This movement also demanded some form of legislative assembly elected by the people as a whole.

The liberals in both the unions and the *zemstva* were in general agreement about their objectives and, by the middle of 1905, were becoming increasingly confident about the prospects of reform. The Social-Democrats, however, benefited less from the deterioration in the country's internal condition. Their leaders, including Lenin, were mostly abroad and their energies were mainly devoted to quarrelling among themselves on matters of socialist doctrine and tactics. For both groups — Bolsheviks and Mensheviks — the liberals were not to be trusted, and the 'bourgeois' revolution which they might bring about was only the first stage in the path to the 'dictatorship of the proletariat'. They played little part in the events of 1905.

The Socialist Revolutionaries, who also stood for the overthrow of the Tsarist régime but who did not accept the teachings of Marx on social and economic questions, were much more actively involved in the country's political life, many of their number playing an active part in the liberal movement. But they continued to advocate the use of terror and assassination to force the monarchy to yield. In July they added Count Shuvalov, Military Governor of Moscow, to their long list of victims.

The Tsar and his advisers were not greatly moved by

Right: *An artist's impression of the mutineers on the* Potemkin *shooting the officers. Once the ship was in their hands they had little idea of what to do with it and sailed to Rumania*

all these signs of a rising political temper among the ordinary people and the educated classes. They appeared to think that procrastination and evasion of the main issues were the best remedies for dealing with a situation which they only dimly appreciated. They had, in any case, no constructive plans to offer.

Nicholas's first public reaction to the events of Bloody Sunday was ambiguous. On 3rd March he issued a manifesto reaffirming faith in the autocracy, condemning all who broke its 'fundamental laws', and calling on 'all right-thinking people of all classes and condition' to rally round their monarch. At the same time he issued a *ukaz* to the Senate proclaiming the right of every citizen to make his complaints and views heard and ordering the Council of Ministers to receive proposals for improving the people's well-being. He also issued a rescript to Bulygin announcing his intention of convoking a sort of consultative assembly – something which, on his accession, he had flatly condemned. None of these acts, contradictory and confusing as they were, made any very deep impression on liberal opinion, and when in August, Bulygin issued the regulations governing the proposed elections to the 'State Duma', as the consultative body was to be called, they were treated with scorn. The electoral system was so obviously arranged to keep representation of the workers and intellectuals to a minimum that the liberals decided to boycott or destroy the new institution.

The act which perhaps did most of all to encourage the opposition and let revolutionary ideas be heard was the granting of autonomy to the universities at the end of August. This immediately turned the university lecture halls into centres of almost continuous political debate and revolutionary oratory. The students and their teachers were joined by factory workers and even soldiers at meetings where the Tsarist régime was denounced and plans for replacing it openly discussed. These were perhaps the first 'teach-ins' of the century.

By the autumn of 1905 political tempers were running very high – far higher than the complacent officials of the government realized. The protest movement was growing and people of all classes were becoming daily less fearful of speaking their minds. The explosion was not long delayed.

Left: *Workers outside the gates of the Putilov works during the strike.* **Top left:** *Troops guard the mail during the St Petersburg strike.* **Bottom left:** *A photograph of members of the first-known workers' Soviet set up by strikers at Ivanovo-Voznesensk*

Chapter 6
General Strike and Workers' Soviet

Count Witte spent much of the year 1905 abroad, where he negotiated the peace settlement with Japan. When he returned to Russia in the autumn he was appalled at the state he found the country in. 'After the January disaster,' he wrote, 'events followed with ominous rapidity, and by September 1905, when I returned from my peace mission in America, the revolution was in full swing.' It was not long after his return that Nicholas found himself obliged to turn, though reluctantly, to Witte as the only states-man capable of dealing with the increasingly alarming situation. Witte himself recalls:

'I assumed the duty of ruling the Russian Empire as President of the Committee of Ministers in October 1905. At that time the country was in a state of complete and universal confusion. The government was in a quandary, and when the revolution boiled up furiously from the depths the authorities were completely paralyzed. They either did nothing or pulled in opposite directions, so that the existing régime and its noble standard-bearer were almost completely swept out of existence. The rioting grew more fierce, not daily but hourly. The revolution came out openly on the streets and assumed an ever more threatening nature. It carried all classes of the population along with it.'

Witte was perhaps not averse, in retrospect, to exaggerating the gravity of the situation which he was summoned to deal with and which he handled with considerable skill and firmness. But there is plenty of evidence to suggest that his picture of Russia in 1905 is very close to the truth. The country was literally seething with revolt, which flared up into a genuinely 'revolutionary situation' in October.

The discontent was by no means limited to the towns and the industrial workers; it affected the peasantry in practically every part of the Russian Empire. After the inevitable lull during the summer months, peasant disorders broke out again on an even larger and more frightening scale in the autumn. Encouraged in their

Left: Students demonstrate on the quayside at St Petersburg

protests by what they heard of the political mood of the people in the towns and by the programme being drawn up by the new Peasants' Union, the peasants began to take the law into their own hands. Though not concentrated in such great numbers or so well organized as the factory workers, the peasantry had the advantage of being remote from the centres of power and authority. The landowners and their agents were hopelessly outnumbered and could put up no effective resistance once the peasants went on the rampage.

Typical of the mood of the simple peasants at the time is this declaration recorded in the province of Kazan:

'The government keeps us peasants down. But the fault is with the Romanovs; the Tsar has sold Russia to Japan. For three hundred years the Romanovs have done nothing for the peasants, and the dukes do nothing but drink. As for us, we have no one to place our hopes in, and we must take all we can by force.'

Spontaneous as it was in many places, the peasant movement was not completely uncontrolled or without organization. A Russian reporter described in his paper, the *Russkiye Vyedomosty,* at the time a typical local 'peasant revolt'. The peasants, he said, would first order the landowner and his family out of his house. Then they would seize his corn and other produce, his livestock, and sometimes his furniture. Then they would dismiss his farmhands and servants, and finally they would burn down the farm buildings. The land from the estate would be handed over to the village commune for distribution in equal plots among the peasants in the following spring. Throughout this procedure, the reporter said, 'the police remain in hiding, or sometimes they are arrested by the peasants'. The peasants told him that their reasons for burning down the farm buildings were twofold: in the first place it meant that the landowner could not return to his estate and undo the peasants' 'reform'; and secondly it deprived the Cossack troops who might be sent against the peasants of comfortable billets.

The newspaper summarized the situation in the central provinces of Russia in the following terms:

'Hundreds of buildings worth several millions of roubles have been destroyed. All the buildings have been razed to the ground in such enormous estates as those of the Duke of Leuchtenberg and Prince Vyazemsky, and such palatial country houses as Prince Prozorovsky's and Demidov's. Many houses have been burned down without reference to the relations which had existed between the peasants and the landowners or to the latter's political views. The farms of such well-known *zemstvo* liberals as Lvov, Yermolayev, and Veselovsky have suffered along with the others. Dozens of old country houses containing

valuable libraries and collections of pictures have been burnt down. Very few of the estates in the Balashev, Atkarsk, Petrovsk, and Serdobsk districts have escaped.'

The reign of anarchy

By October it was clear that the whole social structure and administration of the country districts had broken down, and the government did not have adequate resources to restore order. It was overwhelmed by the demands for assistance, which meant armed force, which poured in from every province. From Tambov the Marshal of the Nobility cabled: 'The province is in danger; over thirty country houses have been burned and looted; every day news of fresh destruction comes in; such measures as were possible have been taken, but troops are few and some of them have been recalled.'

From the same district the local *zemstvo* board, usually liberal in its views, sent a desperate appeal: 'The method of persuasion is without effect on the masses; what is required is troops and the immediate introduction of martial law.'

More than twenty landowners, including some of the best-known names in Russian society, sent the following appeal from the Penza region:

'Country houses are being burned and looted; agitators go around in army uniforms; there is no protection; few troops; we urgently beg you to place more army units and cossacks at our disposal; we implore help, otherwise the province will be utterly devastated.'

But the authorities in the towns and in Petersburg were in no position to send reinforcements. Durnovo, the Minister of the Interior, could reply only with an admission of his own impotence:

'Unfortunately all my requests for troops to be despatched are ineffective, because there simply are no troops available in the empire. You must make do for the present with what you have. Act drastically and harshly.'

This was, of course, cold comfort for the besieged landowners, many of whom saw no alternative to selling up their estates as fast as they could and abandoning their property to its fate.

The destruction brought about by this peasant war was by no means all the work of the peasants themselves. The authorities did not hesitate to take reprisals on the peasants' houses when the opportunity occurred. Later, in 1906, when the situation swung in favour of the authorities, Durnovo advised the governor of Kursk: 'To put an end to the disorders take the most ruthless measures; it will be found useful to raze the rebellious

Left: *An engraving of peasants wrecking a landlord's estate*

villages to the ground and to exterminate the rebels by force of arms without mercy.'

The Russian people were indulging in one of their periodic orgies of self-destruction, and the Russian land was, as usual, suffering in consequence. But it was not just a question of peasant discontent. There were plenty of other sources of trouble for the Tsar's régime; two of the principal ones were the many millions of non-Russians who resented the alien rule, and the hundreds of thousands of soldiers returning slowly from the war in the Far East with few laurels and precious little else to their names. Both categories tended to add fuel to the flames of peasant unrest. Witte himself recalled how the non-Russian population 'seeing this great upheaval, lifted their heads and decided that the time was ripe for the realization of their dreams and desires. The Poles wanted autonomy, the Jews wanted equal rights, and so on. All of them longed for the destruction of the system of deliberate oppression which embittered their lives. And, on top of everything, the army was in an ugly mood.'

The morale of the soldiers had been brought very low by the defeats in the East and their manifestly incapable leadership. Now discontent was increased by the government's reluctance to carry out its promise of speedy demobilization. The result was mutinies in many regiments and occasional pitched battles. Reports of disorders of this kind came in from places as far apart as Grodno and Samara, Rostov and Kursk, from Rembertow near Warsaw, from Riga in Latvia and Vyborg in Finland, from Vladivostok and Irkutsk.

By the autumn the revolutionary movement in the navy had also gained strength, with the result that a mutiny broke out at Kronstadt naval base in the Baltic in October which was put down only by the use of force. It was followed by yet another mutiny in the Black Sea fleet, at Sevastopol, which at one point threatened to take control of the whole city.

The troubles in the armed forces, like those among the peasantry, suffered, from the point of view of the revolutionaries, from the same weaknesses: they were completely unco-ordinated, they lacked capable leaders, and, though they sometimes voiced general political demands, they lacked any clear purpose beyond the satisfaction of their immediate needs. They were outbursts of rage, rather than the actions of a revolutionary movement. But there was no mistaking the violence or bitterness.

The mood of the population in the non-Russian provinces was even more hostile, and there were disorders in the Baltic states, Poland, Finland, the Ukraine, and

Left: *Police search a suspect during unrest in Warsaw*

the Caucasus. But the authorities were generally better prepared for dealing with disaffection in those areas. In Poland, for example, there were never less than 400,000 Russian troops stationed. Most of the Baltic states were put under martial law during the summer of 1905. Ten thousand troops sent as a punitive force to Georgia were not sufficient to bring peace to the region. Discontent in Finland finally took the form of a general strike and forced substantial concessions out of the government.

These disorders among the peasants, non-Russian peoples of the empire, and the returning soldiery were undoubtedly grave. But they were not of themselves capable of presenting a major threat to the very foundations of the Tsarist régime. Such waves of unrest had swept across the country before and dealt with in the only way the Tsarist rulers knew, had eventually subsided. The unrest of 1905 would doubtless have been overcome in the same way had it not been for a new factor in the political situation—the industrial workers, who were beginning for the first time to feel their strength. As Russian society was becoming increasingly concentrated in the towns and dependent on the more complicated techniques and organization of modern industry, so it was also putting itself ever more into the hands of the working people. The peasants and the soldiers could cause the government a great deal of trouble, but they could not bring the towns and the industrial areas to a standstill. The workers could, and that is what they did in 1905. It was they who produced the revolution of 1905.

The general strike of October 1905 came about spontaneously, without leaders and without any co-ordinated plan. It started at the end of September in Moscow, where some printers came out on strike in support of a very modest wage claim. When the employers resisted the claim the Printers' Union called out all the printing workers in the city, and within a week they had been joined by the bakers, carpenters, fitters, textile workers, and railwaymen and the strike began to assume a more general political character. Students from the university linked up with the workers and supported them in their clashes with the police and soldiers who were used to maintain order. By the middle of October there were some 150 casualties on both sides and the conflict was still unresolved.

The printing workers of St Petersburg then decided to come out in sympathy with their colleagues in Moscow, and they were quickly joined by the workers in other industries in what was undisguisedly a political action. Workers, students, and intellectuals met together in the capital at meetings at which far-reaching political demands were formulated and tempers roused.

But it was the workers of Moscow who finally took the action which made the strike general. On 20th October they were led to believe (wrongly, as it turned out) that some railwaymen sent as delegates to an official conference in St Petersburg had been arrested. This was sufficient to persuade all the employees at Moscow's railway junction to come out on strike. Two days later all rail traffic through Moscow was at a standstill.

From that point the strike snowballed rapidly. Within a few days Moscow was cut off from the rest of the country and most of the city's industry and public services were brought to a halt. From Moscow the strike spread along the railway line to Kharkov, where the same sequence of events was repeated: students joined forces with the factory workers, demonstrations led to clashes with the police, to barricades and bloodshed.

The strike spreads rapidly

By the end of October the fire had really taken a hold and there was no stopping it. The railway strike spread to St Petersburg on 25th October and within the next day or two practically every employee in the city had joined in, whether he was in industry, in an office, or in the government service. Even the schoolchildren joined the movement.

The strike then quickly became general, spreading throughout the empire, so that by the last days of October the whole railway system, which then amounted to more than 40,000 miles of railway, was at a standstill, and life in most large cities, especially those with an industry of any importance, came to a halt. Even Peterhof, where the Tsar was staying at the time, could be reached only by sea from St Petersburg. And it was from there that, as usual in time of trouble, Nicholas summoned Witte.

There is no better reflection of the situation in the country in October 1905 than the account of it given by Nicholas himself in a letter to his mother, Maria Fyodorovna. Writing from Peterhof, he recalled the 'January days, which we spent together at Tsarskoye'.

'They were bad enough, weren't they?' he says. 'But they were *nothing* in comparison with the days we are living through now.'

He recalls the various meetings which had taken place in Moscow. 'There they prepared everything for strikes on the railways, which started around Moscow and then spread at once throughout Russia.

'Petersburg and Moscow then found themselves cut off from the provinces. Today it is a whole week since the Baltic line was working. The only way of getting to the

Left: Workers on one of the first barricades to appear in Moscow

ity is by sea – how do you like that at this time of year? From the railways the strike spread to the factories and workshops, and then even to the city administration and the Ministry of Communications. Just imagine, what a scandal! Poor little Khilkov [Minister of Communications] is in despair, but he just can't cope.

'God knows what has been going on in the universities! All sorts of riff-raff have been coming in from the streets, frightful things have been said in speeches, and nobody does anything about it! The college and university councils, once they had got their autonomy, didn't know how to use it. They weren't even able to close their doors against the uncontrolled crowd and then, of course, they complained to the police that they didn't help them (do you remember what they used to say in the old days?).

'It has become really disagreeable to read telegrams from agents, which are full of nothing but reports of strikes in colleges and pharmacies and so forth, of the murder of policemen, Cossacks, and soldiers, of all kinds of disorder, unrest, and alarms. Meanwhile my precious ministers have been meeting together like a lot of frightened children and discussing how to unite all the ministries instead of taking firm action.

'When the people decided openly at their "meetings" (the new fashionable word) to start an armed uprising and I got to know about it, I immediately had all the troops of the Petersburg garrison put under Trepov's command and ordered him to split the city up into sections with a separate commander for each section. Orders have been given for the troops to open fire immediately in the event of an attack on them. This alone put a stop to the movement or the revolution, because Trepov warned that any disorder would be suppressed without mercy – and, of course, everybody believed it.'

But police action by 'honest Trepov', whom Nicholas described as 'irreplaceable, a sort of secretary', was by no means sufficient to hold back the tide of popular pressure. It was no longer a question of simply frightening the population into the familiar state of docility. The working people had acquired for the first time a central forum where their demands could be given shape and which could offer a direct challenge to the government. This was the St Petersburg Soviet of Workers' Deputies which first met on 26th October 1905. The Soviet, or Council, came into being more or less spontaneously, perhaps on the model of the Ivanovo-Voznesensk Soviet, as a rough and ready form of political organization for a people who had practically no institutions through which they could express their demands and no effective political party.

Right: The streets of Kronstadt after the mutiny was suppressed

There were no more than thirty or forty delegates present at the Soviet's first meeting. But before long their number had risen to hundreds, with each delegate, or deputy, nominally representing 500 workers. At the height of its influence the Soviet counted 562 delegates who certainly represented most of the main industrial establishments in the capital, though it was never clear just how much actual power or control the leaders of the Soviet exercized over the working people. It served as a magnificent tribunal for fiery orators, of whom one of the most effective was Lev Trotsky who had returned secretly to Russia in the course of the year and who, like a majority on the Soviet, then favoured the Menshevik point of view. Within a few days of coming into existence the Soviet issued an official bulletin which it called *Izvestia* (meaning 'news') – forerunner of the daily newspaper now published by the Soviet government.

It was not long before other Russian cities, including Moscow, followed the example of the St Petersburg workers and also set up their 'Soviets'. But, with the whole country in the throes of a general strike, there could be little co-ordinated action or organization on a national scale, and the Soviet in the capital remained the spearhead of what appeared to be a nationwide rebellion against the government's authority. For several weeks the Petersburg Soviet enjoyed a semi-official status and was recognized by the government as the only body which could arrange for some of the city's services to resume operation on a limited scale. For this brief period the Soviet appeared to be an alternative centre of political power, the expression of a sort of 'grass-roots' democracy, an experience of which the revolutionaries were to take advantage to carry through a revolution a decade later.

This brief period, which lasted through the greater part of November 1905, marked the crest of the wave of popular revolt and it was this situation that has come to be known as the 'revolution' of 1905. Russia's economy was paralyzed, the nation's administration had broken down, the government was temporarily helpless, and the peoples of the Russian empire were in a state of open revolt against the monarchy. But it was not yet the end of the monarchy, shaken though it was; the system still had enough strength in it to restore its authority, and the forces of reform and revolution were still too divided and disorganized to attempt to take power.

The man who did more than any other to save Tsarism and to whom the Tsar now appealed from Peterhof was Witte, now raised to the rank of Count as a reward for his work on the Japanese peace treaty.

Left: *The court martial of the men who mutinied at Kronstadt*

Chapter 7
Witte and the October Manifesto

'One of the things that have been held against me,' said Witte in his memoirs, 'is that during my premiership I did not shoot enough people and kept others from indulging in that sport. Whoever hesitates to shed blood, it was argued, should not hold so responsible a post as I did. But for my part I consider it to my credit that in the six months when I was in power only a few dozen people were killed in St Petersburg and no one executed.'

Whatever his motives Witte certainly avoided bloodshed as far as he could and tried to apply political skill and statesmanship to the chaotic situation with which he was confronted. He was a pragmatist who recognized that the situation had gone too far to be resolved by the further use of force. Recalling in one of his letters to his mother the long talks he had with Witte after the latter became Prime Minister – 'our talks began in the morning and ended in the evening after dark' – Nicholas recorded the choice with which Witte confronted him: either 'to appoint an energetic military man and try with all the force at our disposal to put the sedition down. This would give us a breathing space, and then in a few months' time we should have to use force again. But this would mean shedding rivers of blood and it would lead in the end back to the present position. . . .

Or, Nicholas explained, 'to grant civil rights to the population – the freedom of speech, of the press, of assembly, and association and the inviolability of the person, and, apart from that, an undertaking to submit every legislative proposal to the State Duma, which means in effect a constitution. Witte argued vigorously in favour of this course, saying that, although it involved some risk, it was the only possible one at the present moment. Practically everyone I asked gave me the same answer as Witte and took the view that there was no other way out. He told me straight that if I wanted to appoint him Prime Minister I would have to accept his programme and not interfere with his actions.'

Left: An artist's impression of Moscow burning as troops move in to suppress the workers. Large areas were reduced to rubble

Nothing could have made clearer the relationship between the weak, vacillating Tsar and the decisive, tough statesman. Nicholas's account of his final capitulation reveals his uncertainty and his fears:

'The manifesto was drawn up by him [Witte] and Alexei Obolensky. We discussed it for two days and then, at last, having offered up a prayer, I signed it. My dear mother, you cannot imagine how much I went through before I did it! I could not explain to you in a telegram all the circumstances which brought me to this frightful decision, which I have nevertheless taken quite deliberately. The whole of Russia seemed to be shouting and writing and begging for it. . . .'

The document which Nicholas signed on 30th October 1905, and which came to be known as the 'October Manifesto', was brief and to the point. But it marked a turning point in Russian history in that the Tsar had at last conceded the principle of popular control over his power. He had handed over to an elected assembly of the people in words at least a portion of the absolute power which he had sworn to preserve intact. The 'senseless dreams' of the people for a constitution had become a reality after all. It was a major retreat by the Russian monarchy, even if the next decade was to see Nicholas and his advisers doing their best to regain the lost ground.

The manifesto opened in the traditional manner:

We, Nicholas the Second, by the grace of God, Emperor and Autocrat of All Russia, Tsar of Poland, Grand Duke of Finland, etc., etc., declare to all our loyal subjects:

Disturbances and unrest in the capitals and many other places in Our Empire fill Our Heart with great and painful grief. The welfare of the Russian Sovereign is indissolubly bound up with the welfare of the people, and their grief is His grief. Out of the present disturbances may develop serious popular disorder, and a threat to the integrity and unity of Our Empire. . . .

Therefore, Nicholas announced, he had ordered the government:

Firstly: to grant the people the fundamental civil liberties;
Secondly: to admit immediately to participation in the State Duma . . . those classes of the population which are now completely deprived of electoral rights, leaving the further extension of the principle of universal suffrage to the new legislature. [This meant in practice to make good the shortcomings in the 'Bulygin Duma' by which whole classes of the population had been deprived of the right to vote directly.]

Left: *Troops amid the wreckage in the streets of Kronstadt after the last vestiges of resistance had finally been crushed*

Thirdly: to establish as an inviolable rule that no law may become effective without the consent of the State Duma. [The Duma was also to have control over officials appointed by the Tsar.]

We call on all faithful sons of Russia, the Tsar said in conclusion, *to remember their duty to their Fatherland, to assist in putting an end to these unprecedented disturbances, and to make with Us every effort to restore peace and quiet to Our native land.*

The manifesto did not, however, have the immediate effect of calming the country down. On the contrary, there was wide-spread excitement, some rejoicing, and much demonstrating. Large sections of the population appeared to believe that a major battle had been won against the powers of autocracy, and there were many liberal politicians and intellectuals who believed the same. But there were as many who saw the manifesto only as the first encouraging step in a long battle, and many more who suspected the Tsar, or at least Witte, of insincerity and of having little intention of fulfilling the manifesto's promises. Conservative circles were utterly appalled at what Nicholas had done with practically no consultation with his advisers and ministers.

The revolutionaries, still intoxicated by the flow of speeches in the Petersburg Soviet and sailing along on the wave of popular protest, treated the manifesto with open contempt. For Trotsky, writing in *Izvestia,* the document was pure deception and a cover for more brutality to come:

'Witte has come, but Trepov still remains . . . The working people know what they want and what they do not want. They do not want either Trepov, the police thug, or Witte, the liberal financial shark—neither the wolf's snout nor the fox's tail. They reject the police truncheon wrapped up in a constitution.'

Lenin took a similar view. Denouncing the manifesto as a 'scrap of paper', he said it was intended only to prepare for a struggle against the revolution.

The main significance of the manifesto was that it introduced a new element into the confused and dangerous situation, in which for so long nothing had changed. Although initially it made confusion only more confused, its ultimate effect was, as Witte no doubt intended, to take the fire out of the revolutionary movement.

The promise, made in the manifesto, that civil liberties would be respected henceforth was not accompanied by any formal legislation to guarantee those liberties, so that the authorities were uncertain how to react to the continuing state of disorder. It was not long before the more reactionary elements in society stepped in to supplant the forces of law and order, to defend the mon-

archy, and do battle with the liberals and revolutionaries. Bands of such people, eagerly joined by young rowdies and criminals, but often enjoying also the backing of the clergy and the police, who were known as the 'Black Hundreds', attacked revolutionaries, students, nationalist Poles, Finns, and, above all, the Jews. In the first half of November Russia was swept by a wave of anti-Semitic pogroms as violent as it had ever seen. The worst took place in Odessa, where for three whole days nationalist gangs roamed through the Jewish parts of the city, attacking and killing people and destroying buildings, while the police and troops stood aside from the conflict. At least five hundred people lost their lives in this disgraceful episode – hardly a good beginning to the new era of civil liberty. The Jews were the principal victims in many other cities, but in the Caucasus it was the Armenians who suffered most and in many places it was Russian opponents of the régime who suffered at the hands of the Black Hundreds.

The revolution loses momentum
Nicholas reported to his mother on the pogroms without any apparent regrets:

'In the days immediately following the issue of the manifesto bad elements caused a great deal of trouble, but then followed a strong reaction against them and the whole mass of loyal citizens swung into action.

'The result was what you might have expected: as usual in Russia the people became indignant at the brazen, insolent way the revolutionaries and socialists were behaving, and, since nine-tenths of them are Jews, the whole of their anger was concentrated on them. Hence the Jewish pogroms. It was amazing that this happened simultaneously and immediately in all the towns of Russia and Siberia. Of course, in England they are saying that the disorders were organized by the police – it's always the same old story! But it wasn't only the Jews who caught it. Russian agitators, engineers, lawyers, and all sorts of unpleasant characters also suffered.'

And, with a striking absence of emotion, Nicholas added:

'Incidents in Tomsk, Simferopol, Tver, and Odessa showed clearly to what extremes an enraged crowd can go. They surrounded houses in which revolutionaries had locked themselves and set fire to them, killing anybody who tried to get out.'

Despite the continuing unrest, however, the truth was that, for a variety of reasons, the revolutionary movement was losing some of its momentum, and this in turn

Left: The 'Black Hundreds', leaders of reaction, on the march

93

affected the policy of the Petersburg Soviet and its leaders. They had been swept into power and prominence by the largely spontaneous strike movement and they were still at the mercy of the mood among the population. Their first reaction to the October Manifesto was to declare that the general strike would go on. But the people themselves, possibly appeased somewhat by the promise of political reform and with their ardour damped by lack of earnings, began to return to work, and the Soviet was forced on 3rd November to call the strike off. This was admittedly a tactical move, aimed at retaining leadership of the working people; the next move, they said, would be an armed uprising, for which they had started to make plans. But in fact, when, on 14th November, they called another general strike, there was so little response that they had to call it off a few days later.

Meanwhile Witte was biding his time. The fact that the manifesto had resulted in increased unrest rather than the reverse had exposed him to much criticism from the monarchist and conservative circles. But he worked on the assumption that the promise of a constitution and of respect for civil liberties, which had been the most commonly voiced demands throughout the year, would in the end quieten the revolutionary ardour of the masses and weaken the position of their leaders. So he waited for the authority of the Petersburg Soviet to decline before he entered on a trial of strength with its leaders.

Witte strikes at the Soviet

On 30th November the proposal to call a general strike was again debated at a meeting of the Soviet and was rejected for lack of support. The Soviet was also obliged to drop its plan for forcing the employers to accept an eight-hour day. Witte judged that the Soviet was rapidly losing whatever authority it had had over the working people, and he decided to strike. 'It was then,' he recalls, 'that I found it opportune to have Nosar arrested. The arrest was made on 9th December.' Nosar was the President of the Soviet, a Jewish lawyer of Menshevik views who was known in political life under the name of Khrustalev.

The Soviet immediately elected a new committee of three, of whom Trotsky was one, to carry on its work, while the Soviet itself met less frequently. But Witte did not intend to allow it to regain its authority. Once he

Bottom right: Count Witte and the manifesto which he drew up for the Tsar (top right). It did not succeed in calming the country and its appearance was followed by more demonstrations (right) and finally by an armed rising of the workers in Moscow

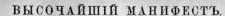

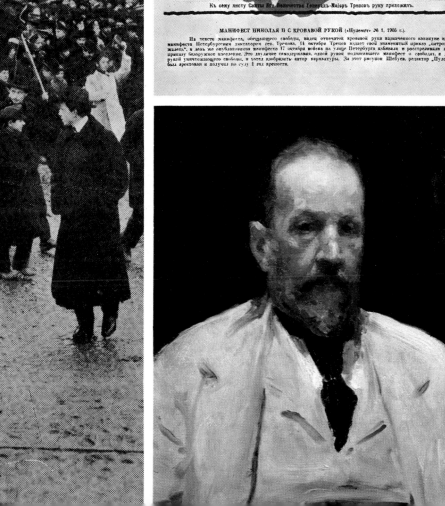

ВЫСОЧАЙШІЙ МАНИФЕСТЪ.

БОЖІЕЮ МИЛОСТІЮ,

МЫ, НИКОЛАЙ ВТОРЫЙ,

ИМПЕРАТОРЪ И САМОДЕРЖЕЦЪ ВСЕРОССІЙСКІЙ,

ЦАРЬ ПОЛЬСКІЙ, ВЕЛИКІЙ КНЯЗЬ ФИНЛЯНДСКІЙ,

и прочая, и прочая, и прочая.

Смуты и волненія въ столицахъ и во многихъ мѣстностяхъ Имперіи Нашей великою и тяжкою скорбью преисполняютъ сердце Наше. Благо Россійскаго Государя неразрывно съ благомъ народнымъ и печаль народная—Его печаль. Отъ волненій, нынѣ возникшихъ, можетъ явиться глубокое нестроеніе народное и угроза цѣлости и единству Державы Нашей.

Великій обѣтъ Царскаго служенія повелѣваетъ Намъ всѣми силами разума и власти Нашей стремиться къ скорѣйшему прекращенію столь опасной для Государства смуты. Повелѣвъ подлежащимъ властямъ принять мѣры къ устраненію прямыхъ проявленій безпорядка, безчинствъ и насилій, въ охрану людей мирныхъ, стремящихся къ спокойному выполненію лежащаго на каждомъ долга, Мы, для успѣшнѣйшаго выполненія общихъ предначертанныхъ Нами къ умиротворенію государственной жизни мѣръ, признали необходимымъ объединить дѣятельность высшаго Правительства.

На обязанность Правительства возлагаемъ Мы выполненіе непреклонной Нашей воли:

1. Даровать населенію незыблемыя основы гражданской свободы на началахъ дѣйствительной неприкосновенности личности, свободы совѣсти, слова, собраній и союзовъ.

2. Не останавливая предназначенныхъ выборовъ въ Государственную Думу, привлечь теперь же къ участію въ Думѣ, въ мѣрѣ возможности соотвѣтствующей краткости остающагося до созыва Думы срока, тѣ классы населенія, которые нынѣ совсѣмъ лишены избирательныхъ правъ, предоставивъ засимъ дальнѣйшее развитіе начала общаго избирательнаго права вновь установленному законодательному порядку,

и 3. Установить, какъ незыблемое правило, чтобы никакой законъ не могъ воспріять силу безъ одобренія Государственной Думы и чтобы выборнымъ отъ народа обезпечена была возможность дѣйствительнаго участія въ надзорѣ за закономѣрностью дѣйствій поставленныхъ отъ Насъ властей.

Призываемъ всѣхъ вѣрныхъ сыновъ Россіи вспомнить долгъ свой передъ Родиною, помочь прекращенію сей неслыханной смуты и вмѣстѣ съ Нами напрячь всѣ силы къ возстановленію тишины и мира на родной землѣ.

Данъ въ Петергофѣ, въ 17-й день октября въ лѣто отъ Рождества Христова тысяча девятьсотъ пятое, Царствованія же Нашего одиннадцатое.

На подлинномъ Собственною Его Императорскаго Величества рукою подписано:

"НИКОЛАЙ".

Къ сему листу Свиты Его Величества Генералъ-Маіоръ Треповъ руку приложилъ.

МАНИФЕСТЪ НИКОЛАЯ II С КРОВАВОЙ РУКОЙ («Пулеметъ» № 1, 1905 г.).

На текстѣ манифеста, обѣщающаго свободы, видны отпечатки кровавой руки казначеено́го изданіе над манифеста Петербургскимъ диктаторомъ ген. Треповымъ. 14 октября Треповъ издаетъ свой знаменитый приказъ "патроновъ не жалѣть", и въ день обнародованія манифеста 17 октября войска на улицѣ Петербурга избивали и разстрѣливали по приказу безоружное населеніе. Это двуличіе самодержавія, одной рукой подписывающаго манифестъ о свободахъ, а другой рукой уничтожающаго свободы, и хотѣлъ изобразить авторъ каррикатуры. За этотъ рисунокъ Шебуевъ, редакторъ "Пулемета", былъ арестованъ и получилъ по суду 1 годъ крѣпости.

was sure that he was right in his belief that the workers were losing interest in the fate of the Soviet and he saw that there was no serious protest at Nosar's arrest, he ordered Durnovo, the Minister of the Interior, to arrest the whole Soviet. On 16th December the building of the Free Economic Society in which the Soviet was meeting was quickly surrounded by police, gendarmes, Cossacks, and guards, and all the members of the Soviet present — some 200 of them, including most of the members of the Executive Committee — were arrested.

(Only fifty-two of the arrested deputies were eventually put on trial, of whom only fifteen, including Trotsky, were sentenced to be deported to Siberia for life. Trotsky escaped on the way to Siberia, returned briefly to Petersburg, and then emigrated abroad. Lenin, who had not played a prominent part in the work of the Soviet, remained in hiding and moved to Finland in 1907.)

That was the end of the Petersburg Soviet, but not the end of the revolution. There was to be one final and bloody clash before the year 1905 came to an end.

On the eve of their arrest the deputies to the Soviet had issued a manifesto calling upon the population to declare a financial war on the government by refusing to pay taxes and withdrawing all bank and savings bank deposits. The government's reply to this challenge had been to close down the eight newspapers which printed the manifesto and institute proceedings against the editors. Then, with the arrest of the Soviet, the radical leaders saw that the government was taking the offensive, and they had hardly any choice but to take up the challenge. The few leaders of the Soviet who were still free, in agreement with the Socialists and Socialist Revolutionaries, issued a call for a general political strike once again, with the Bolsheviks pressing for the strike to be the prelude to an armed uprising against the régime. The appeal met with considerable support, including that of the railway workers, and the scene was set for the decisive trial of strength between the forces of revolution and the forces of what was still in effect autocracy.

As it happened, the battle was fought out in Moscow and not in Petersburg, where the arrest of the Soviet and other signs of the government's determination to act firmly discouraged the workers from responding to the strike appeal. For the first time in 1905, the capital of the empire, which had also given the lead to the revolutionary movement, played only a secondary role. The scene shifted to Moscow, where the strike movement had started in October.

Left: *Death stalks into Moscow. The Tsar's troops put down the rising with great cruelty and thousands were sent into exile*

The workers of Moscow came out on strike on 20th December, and within a few days all industry in the Moscow region was once again at a standstill, the train services halted, the city's administration crippled, and the schools closed down. For a certain time it seemed as though, like the Petersburg Soviet a few weeks previously, the Moscow Soviet, which had remained in existence, was in control of the city. What is more, the leaders of the Soviet entertained serious hopes, which were not without foundation, that the troops of the Moscow garrison would join in the revolt.

According to Witte, 'the whole of Moscow was in either open or secret opposition, including the representatives of the nobility and the merchant class. Some Moscow millionaires contributed liberally, not only to the cause of the movement in favour of a constitution, but also to the cause of revolution. Savva Morozov, the industrial magnate, gave the revolutionaries several millions through an actress who lived with Maxim Gorky and with whom Morozov was infatuated.' But it was not, in Witte's view, so much the revolutionary mood of the people of Moscow as the lack of decision on the part of the Governor-General which allowed the situation to get out of hand. 'Ill-informed and inefficient, the authorities shirked their responsibilities, evaded personal dangers, and shrank from fighting the approaching revolution.'

Though he had been the author of the October Manifesto and the advocate of concessions to the liberal movement, Witte was not afraid of asserting the government's authority. Nicholas, who had written to his mother in November: 'I cannot conceal from you a certain disappointment in Witte. Everybody thought that he was such an energetic and despotic man,' was saying in the middle of December: 'Witte will now start to put the revolution down properly – at least, that's what he told me. He realizes that all right-thinking people are dissatisfied with him and were getting impatient with his failure to take action. . . .'

The situation in Moscow was at a stalemate, with neither the Soviet nor the authorities ready to move, until Witte succeeded in persuading the Tsar to appoint a more effective Governor-General, in the person of General Dubasov. He started raiding strike meetings and arresting as many of the leaders as he could. This put the strikers into a more fighting mood and forced them on to the streets, where they started building barricades and fighting pitched battles with the police and troops. For the best part of a week street-fighting continued in the working-class districts of Moscow, but at the end

Left: The reality. The Semyonov regiment reaches the Kremlin

of it the situation was still undecided because, although the troops of the Moscow garrison did not join the strikers, Dubasov was not sure enough of their loyalty to use them against the strikers.

In the end it was Witte who resolved the situation, by persuading the Tsar to order the despatch of reliable troops to Moscow to assist Dubasov. Practically the whole of the crack Semyonov regiment, supported by cavalry and artillery, was sent post-haste from Petersburg, with orders to act with all severity. 'I understand that the insurrection was suppressed unsystematically and with excessive cruelty on the part of the men of the Semyonovsky regiment,' Witte said afterwards.

The Moscow Soviet is crushed

The main battle was fought out in the Presnya district of Moscow, now known as the 'Red' Presnya in recognition of the part it played in those revolutionary days. The workers fought with great courage, but there was never any doubt as to the outcome of the battle. The workers were outnumbered, and it was no longer so clear to them or to others exactly what they were fighting for. Whereas during the October strike the workers appeared to be part of a national movement embracing all classes of the population, in December they seemed to be fighting on their own. They did not have the backing of the rest of the population of the city, and the city itself was cut off from the rest of the country. Though there were strikes and up risings in other cities of the empire, they were not sufficient to bring the country's economy to a standstill. Moreover, in December, the peasants, though still in a state of revolt, showed no interest in the activities of the Moscow factory workers.

The Moscow Soviet was soon forced to acknowledge defeat, with an announcement that the strike would end at the end of December. Losses in the battle were substantial; hundreds of people lost their lives either in the fighting or in summary executions at the hands of the military. Thousands were arrested and sent to Siberia. Large areas of Moscow had been reduced to rubble.

The defeat of the Moscow uprising was in fact the end of the revolution of 1905. On the whole it may be seen as an ill-judged attempt to keep the fires of revolution burning too long after the fuel had run out. The uprising had been in the main inspired by the Bolsheviks. Other groups of radicals had hesitated and shared the view later expressed by Russia's leading Marxist Georgi Plekhanov, that the strike had been premature and that 'there was no need to take up arms'.

Left: Presnya; armed workers march off to fight the Tsar's troops

Lenin hotly contested this point of view. He argued that the main lesson of the Moscow uprising was that the working people were *more* revolutionary than the men who claimed to lead them, and that the fault lay in the leaders who were unprepared for the uprising and unable to lead it to a successful conclusion. 'The organizations lagged behind the growth and scope of the movement,' he said.

'The proletarian struggle of the masses went over the heads of the organizations from a strike to an uprising. In this we see an enormous historical acquisition of the Russian revolution, achieved in December 1905 – an acquisition bought, like all the earlier ones, at the cost of tremendous sacrifices.

'The movement was raised from the level of a general political strike to a higher level. It forced the reaction to go to the extreme in resisting it and in so doing it brought a gigantic step nearer the moment when the revolution will also go to the extreme in its use of means of attack.

'The reaction cannot go any farther than shooting down barricades, houses, and street crowds. But the revolution can go a lot farther than did the Moscow fighters, much, much farther, both in scope and in depth. The revolution moved a lot farther ahead with December. The basis of the revolutionary crisis became immeasurably wider – now the knife must be made even sharper.'

And, taking up Plekhanov's judgment, Lenin declared:

'On the contrary, they should have taken up arms with greater determination, more energetically, and more aggressively; they should have explained to the masses the impossibility of having only a peaceful strike and the need for fearless and merciless armed struggle. . . . To conceal from the masses the need for a desperate, bloody, and annihilating war as the immediate task of the future would be to deceive both ourselves and the people.'

That, as far as Lenin was concerned, was the first lesson of the December uprising. But subsequent events did not bear out his reading of the situation. The uprising was, for the time being, the end and not the beginning.

Encouraged by Dubasov's success with strong-arm methods, the government under Witte proceeded to enforce law and order and to carry out a 'mopping-up' operation throughout the empire. 'Since the events in Moscow, Witte has completely changed. Now he wants to hang and shoot everybody,' Nicholas commented with satisfaction. 'I never saw such a chameleon or a man who changed his views the way he does. Because of this quality practically *nobody* trusts him any more and he has **109** ▷

Right: The beginning of the end; women prisoners off to Siberia
Next page: Witte and his Cabinet rush round in circles getting nowhere. A cartoonist ridicules their attempts to bring peace

The decisive last act

The last act of the 1905 revolution came on 20th December when the workers of Moscow came out on strike and quickly brought the whole city to a halt. The Soviet set up by the strikers was in almost complete control of the city, but unable to use this power to any real advantage because the troops in the city remained loyal to the Tsar and the authorities were unwilling to make any move to meet the demands of the strikers. In the end it was Witte who resolved the stalemate by persuading the Tsar to send in more troops and put down the strikers by force. After fierce fighting, particularly in the Presnya district, the Moscow Soviet was forced to call off the strike. Losses in battle had been considerable — and these were greatly increased by the summary executions which followed **(below)**. Once the rising was over, the Tsar's police and troops rounded up thousands of strikers **(right)** and sent them to Siberia. The opponents of the régime were temporarily in total disarray

finally destroyed himself in everybody's eyes – except, perhaps, in the eyes of foreign Jews.' Nicholas had never enjoyed his relations with the man who had forced him to grant a constitution!

Revolutionary activity in the towns was brought to an end by the banning of most meetings, especially those in the universities, and by police supervision of those which were permitted to take place. Troops were sent out into the provinces to bring order to those regions where the fires of revolt were still burning. There was some heavy fighting in the Baltic states and in Siberia along the Trans-Siberian railway before order was restored. There were occasional outbreaks of insubordination among the troops in Petersburg, Moscow, Kiev, and other centres. The sailors of Sevastopol mutinied under the leadership of Lieutenant Schmidt and the cruiser *Ochakov* was damaged. But by the end of January 1906 life in most parts of the vast empire had returned to normal.

The revolution had been defeated; the revolutionaries were forced into illegality or abroad. But the Tsarist régime did not emerge from the events of 1905 entirely unscathed. Russia was no longer an autocracy but, on paper at least, a constitutional monarchy, and, though the radicals had been defeated, there were still large sections of liberal opinion in the country which wanted to see the promises of the October Manifesto put into practice.

Left: Tsarist generals carouse after the revolt had been crushed

Chapter 8
Parliamentary Aftermath

In October 1905, as we have seen, the whole of Russia was in revolt against the Tsar, and if by the end of the year the tide of dissent and discontent had receded it was primarily because of the October Manifesto, in which Nicholas had promised his people a representative assembly with power to control legislation. Despite the disturbances which had followed the manifesto, the promise still stood and the Tsar and his government were committed to making it good. Between 1906 and 1917 Russia did indeed carry out her first and to this day only experiment in parliamentary democracy. If it can scarcely be described as a very successful experiment and if it foundered ultimately in the tumult of war and revolution, it cannot be dismissed as a complete failure. Russia in 1906, with all her many social and economic problems, her burden of illiteracy and history of autocratic rule, was not the ideal place for the introduction of democratic practices. Nor can it be said that those whose task it was to lead the country along the new paths approached their work with great enthusiasm.

Nicholas, for example, had no intention whatsoever of handing over any of his power to the people. Once the rebellious masses had been brought to order he refused to take the promised reforms very seriously:

'I am having some very serious and tiring conferences this week on the question of the elections to the State Duma,' he wrote. 'Its whole future depends on the solution of this highly important question. Alexei Obolensky and a number of other men have suggested that we should have a general election – that is, universal suffrage. But I turned this down very firmly yesterday. God knows why these gentlemen let their imaginations run so wild!'

Witte was no more enthusiastic than the Tsar for the constitution he had foisted on him. The late Sir Bernard Pares, the historian, recalled asking Witte if he was author of the October Manifesto. 'Certainly,' said Witte.

Left: The scene in the Winter Palace as the Tsar opens the first Duma. The ceremony was deliberately made as brilliant as possible to impress the deputies with the Tsar's power

111

'Then may we regard you as the author of the Constitution?' Pares asked. 'Certainly,' Witte said.

'And what do you think of the Constitution now?' Pares continued.

'I have a Constitution in my head, but, as to my heart, I spit on it!' Witte replied.

'And he spat on the floor in front of me,' Pares added.

Such views were certainly shared by the various right-wing organizations which were gathering strength, such as the Union of the Russian People, the Union of the Russian Land, and the Russian Orthodox Committee, all of which enjoyed support from the Church and sometimes the police.

At the other end of the scale, the Social Democrats and the Socialist Revolutionaries were openly sceptical of the intentions of the Tsar and his advisers. They would not pin their faith on institutions permitted by the monarchy; they were for 'direct action' by their own organizations.

It was primarily the liberals, now more or less united in their own party as 'Constitutional Democrats', or 'Cadets', under the able leadership of Pavel Milyukov, who were genuinely ready to try to make a parliamentary régime work and to turn the new Duma into an effective instrument of popular control. But there were other political parties, less radical than the Cadets, who were also preparing to play their part in the forthcoming elections. Prominent among them were the 'Octobrists' whose policy was based on the fulfilment of the October Manifesto.

The elections were finally announced for March, and the early part of the year was taken up with the election campaign. The electoral system was anything but the 'four-tailed' one (universal, equal, secret, and direct) which the opposition had demanded. All men over the age of twenty-five were given the vote, but only very few — landowners with estates of more than 400 acres — were able to vote directly. Peasants voted indirectly in three stages, choosing delegates to vote at higher levels. The imposition of property qualifications on the urban population meant that only very few factory workers had access to the ballot-box. The system worked in practice

*Top left: The imperial family arrives to attend an early session of the first Duma. Within a month, the Tsar had refused to accept any of the demands of the deputies and the assembly was deadlocked. It was to remain so until the government was able to find a plausible excuse to dissolve it on 21st July. **Bottom left:** The first Duma in action. In spite of attempts by the government to ensure that it would be a 'rubber stamp' for all measures put to it, it contained an overwhelming majority of deputies who were highly critical of the actions of the Tsar and his government*

in such a way as to give the relatively small class of landowners 31 per cent of the votes, while the largest class in the population, the peasants, had 42 per cent, and the towns accounted for 27 per cent.

The elections were to produce a Duma of nearly 500 deputies, of whom 412 would represent the provinces of European Russia, thirty-six would be elected by the Polish provinces, and twenty-nine by the peoples of the Caucasus. The remainder would represent Siberia, Central Asia, and the Far East.

However inadequate this system might appear by present-day standards, it did provide a means of creating a parliament with some claim to represent the interests of the people and to act as a counterweight to the autocracy. It was in any case probably beyond the ability of the authorities to organize a genuinely universal ballot throughout the length and breadth of the Russian empire. In the event, the people themselves took full advantage of their new electoral rights in what turned out to be a lively election campaign, despite the boycott on it declared by the Social Democrats and SRs.

The new Duma's wings are clipped

Even before the elections could be held, however, and before the new Duma came into being, the Tsar pushed through a number of measures, despite strong opposition by Witte, which severely curtailed the rights of the new Duma. Nicholas announced that the existing State Council would be transformed into a sort of upper house sitting alongside the State Duma and enjoying equal rights over the passage of legislation, which would still require the Imperial sanction to become law. The new State Council would be composed in equal numbers of people appointed by the Tsar and people elected by the *zemstva* and professional classes. The new Duma was having its wings clipped even before it came into existence.

There followed further measures in the same vein. The election campaign was hampered by new regulations governing the holding of public meetings. Then it was announced that the Duma would have no control over the expenditure of the Imperial court or over the cost of the army and navy. Finally, on 2nd May, 1906, the Tsar issued a new version of the 'Fundamental Laws' of the Russian state, in which he gave the answer to the question, widely debated since the October Manifesto, as to whether the Tsar's powers had been in any way curtailed. The answer was that they had not.

'The Emperor of All Russia,' the document said, 'has supreme autocratic power. It is ordained by God Himself that his authority should be submitted to, not only out of fear but out of a genuine sense of duty.'

The Fundamental Laws went on to spell out specific attributes of the Emperor's power. He alone could declare war or approve a peace settlement. He was the supreme authority over the Orthodox Church. He could summon or dissolve the Duma at will. He appointed the ministers of the government, and they were responsible to him alone. Even if the Duma, by a two-thirds majority, passed a vote of censure on the government, this did not necessarily involve the government's dismissal.

With these measures, contrary to the spirit and the letter of the October Manifesto, the Tsar had made sure that his own powers could not be restricted in any way by the new 'parliament'. The liberal opposition was correspondingly depressed but none the less determined to do battle on the floor of the new assembly.

On the same day as the new Fundamental Laws were published Witte resigned from the post of prime minister, and, with little hesitation and some relief, Nicholas accepted his resignation. By then Witte was under fire from all directions. Nicholas never forgave him for his role in pressing the October Manifesto on him, and he may well have feared Witte's manifest ability and ambition. The right-wing bureaucrats and politicians were his bitter critics, and the liberals could no longer trust him. Yet it was he who saved the monarchy in 1905, and even on the eve of his resignation he completed negotiations for a loan from France of 2,250 million gold francs, a remarkable feat which did much to strengthen the régime. Of his motives in resigning at this point, Witte said:

'It soon became clear to everyone concerned that the position of the dynasty and of the régime generally was not as insecure as had appeared at first. The revolutionary ardour of the educated proved to be but intellectual itching and the result of idleness. . . .

'As early as January 1906, I told the Grand-Duke Nikolai Nikolayevich that as soon as I had contracted the loan and evacuated Manchuria I would resign my post, for the reason that I found it impossible to play the part of a screen for men and measures I was opposed to. I did not wish to be a cat's-paw for General Trepov and the Grand-Duke Nikolai, or a shield for the Black Hundreds. I resigned in May.'

'I remain unalterably well-disposed towards you and sincerely grateful,' the Tsar wrote to Witte in parting. Of 'Alix', with whom he had never been on good terms, Witte commented:

Left: *Troops stand guard outside the Winter Palace during the opening ceremonies. The establishment of the Duma only temporarily stilled the unrest which had swept across Russia*

'It is said that an exclamation of relief was her only comment on the news of my resignation.'

Witte was succeeded by I. Goremykin, an elderly bureaucrat and an ardent monarchist with nothing but contempt for elected institutions. He was hardly the ideal man to handle the new Duma.

It was, as Witte had predicted and intended, a 'peasant Duma', with peasants accounting for 191 of the deputies and peasant farmers making up the largest professional group. But, to everyone's surprise, instead of constituting a solid block of support for the right wing, the peasants sided almost to a man with the left-wing parties and put up a vigorous battle for a radical solution of the land question. There were altogether twenty-six political parties and sixteen national groups represented in the Duma, but by far the largest number of seats – 184 – was held by the Constitutional Democrats. To the left of these there were more than a hundred deputies of various groups and points of view, including seventeen Socialist Revolutionaries and two Social Democrats, who had been elected despite their parties' non-participation in the electoral campaign. On the other side of the house there were only about fifty deputies with views politically to the right of the Cadets.

The 'opposition Duma'

The most remarkable feature of this new body was that, despite the efforts of the Tsar and the government to make sure that the new Duma would be no more than a rubber stamp for measures submitted to it from above, it turned out in fact to be very much an 'opposition Duma'. It was clear from the outset that any degree of co-operation between the government and the Duma, or at any rate with the dominant Cadet party, would be impossible to achieve. Although there were many differing points of view represented in the Duma, the overwhelming majority of the deputies were highly critical of the Tsar and his ministers. It was not long before they were in conflict.

The opening ceremony, however, passed off without incident. It was not held in the Taurida Palace, where the Duma normally met, but in the Tsar's Winter Palace in Petersburg, on 10th May. It was a brilliant occasion, at which the Tsar and Tsarina appeared with their whole court and ministers in full regalia, calculated presumably to impress the assembled representatives of the people with the imperial majesty. Nicholas gave a brief and generally conciliatory address from the throne.

When, however, the deputies reassembled in their permanent meeting place they were in a fighting mood,

Left: A special meeting of the Constitutional Democrats

117

and almost their first act was to pass, with hardly a
single dissenting voice raised against it, an 'Address to
the Throne' with a long list of far-reaching demands. The
most important of these were: a political amnesty, con-
fiscation of all large estates, ministerial responsibility
to the Duma, the introduction of universal and direct
franchise, the abolition of the Tsar's new State Council,
the abrogation of all emergency laws, the abolition of the
death penalty, and a general reform of the civil service.
This was in fact the full programme of the Constitutional
Democrats, accepted by the whole Duma, which asked to
be allowed to send a deputation to present the Address to
the Tsar in person.

Nicholas refused this request. But towards the end of
May he instructed Goremykin to inform the deputies that
their demands were 'totally inadmissible'. By the time
the Prime Minister had reached the end of his speech the
chamber was in an uproar. The deputies immediately
passed a unanimous vote of no confidence in the government and demanded that it resign immediately. But
the vote and the demand were ignored, and relations
between the Duma and the government were at a deadlock. It was not a good start for the parliamentary system
in Russia.

The first Duma remained in this state of deadlock
throughout the seventy-three days of its life. The deputies
continued to meet and make fiery speeches; the government ignored them, waiting for a convenient excuse to
proclaim the dissolution of the chamber. This it found at
last in the attitude taken up by the Duma on the question
of agrarian reform. The dissolution was proclaimed on
21st July.

Two hundred of the deputies crossed the frontier into
Finland, from where they issued an appeal to the Russian
people to join a campaign of 'passive resistance' to the
government by refusing to pay their taxes or to perform
their military service. The appeal evoked little response
from the population. But it provided the authorities with
an excuse for indicting and sentencing the signatories
of the appeal to prison, which put the Cadet party out of
action as a force in the parliament.

That was in fact the end of Russia's first, fumbling attempt to introduce parliamentary government. Those who
had campaigned so vigorously for a 'constitution' and a representative assembly seemed to be little moved by its

*Top right: Goremykin (left), Witte's successor as prime min-
ister, and Milyukov (right), leader of the Constitutional Democrats. Right: Stolypin, who followed Goremykin as prime
minister, with his family. Bottom right: The spirit of the murdered workers, unappeased by the granting of a new constitution, prophetically cries out for revenge and revolution*

collapse. With the dissolution of the Duma the colourless Goremykin was dismissed and replaced by the more forceful Peter Stolypin, who set about the task of making the Duma serve his and the government's needs. He realized, as Witte had realized before him, that it served no good purpose for the government to set its face against any and every demand for reform. 'As the revolution is so strong,' he said, 'I must carry through effective measures of reform, and at the same time I must face revolution, resist it, and stop it.'

The second Duma, which met from March to June, 1907, was an even more radical body than its predecessor. Lenin, who had opposed participation in the first Duma and believed that armed uprising was imminent, had changed his view, when he saw that the assembly provided a forum for opposition views. Both the Social Democrats and the Socialist Revolutionaries took part in the elections and succeeded between them in electing about a hundred of the new deputies. In addition there were another hundred members of the 'Labour Group', which meant that there were now some 200 deputies to the left of the Cadets, whose numbers had been reduced to ninety-two. The presence of so strong a radical wing did not, however, make the second Duma more effective than the first. Most of its brief life was spent in clashes between Left and Right, and neither wing was particularly interested in making a success of the experiment in parliamentary rule.

Stolypin soon found a device for dissolving the second Duma, and immediately set about reforming the electoral law so as to ensure that future Dumas would contain many more representatives of the wealthy landowning class and nobility and fewer of the 'unreliable' sections of the population and of the non-Russian minorities. By this means the third Duma was dominated by the parties of the Right and proved to be a docile body in the Prime Minister's hands. The fourth Duma was even more conservative in composition. Both bodies were allowed to live their allotted span, and lasted altogether from 1907 to the beginning of 1917. By then Russia was again in the throes of revolution. The next time the Tsarist régime was threatened no one was able to save it.

By then the 'revolutionary year' of 1905 had been forgotten. Indeed, the 'revolution' of 1905 was in fact no revolution at all. It was, as Trotsky said, no more than a 'dress rehearsal' for the revolution to come. The autocracy was shaken but not overthrown. The defenders of the autocracy learnt little or nothing from the events of 1905. Its opponents learnt a great deal.

Left: 'Now at last my people and I are at peace' says the Tsar

Chronology of Events

1861 The emancipation of the serfs by Alexander II
1881 Alexander II assassinated
Alexander III, on his ascent to the throne, affirms his faith in autocratic rule
1894 Nicholas II comes to the throne
1896 Nearly 2,000 people die in a stampede on the Khodynka field when Nicholas II is crowned in Moscow
30th September: the Cassini Convention between Russia and China concerning Manchuria
1898 The Russians are granted a 25-year lease of the Liaotung peninsula
1900 Miners in the Donets basin go on strike
1901 Strikes take place in St Petersburg, Moscow, Ivanovo-Voznesensk, Nizhny-Novgorod, Odessa, Tiflis, Saratov, Astrakhan, and in the Urals
1903 The Russian Social-Democratic Labour Party splits up into the Mensheviks and the Bolsheviks
There is a general strike throughout the southern industrial regions
1904 **8th February:** the Japanese trigger off the Russo-Japanese War when they attack Port Arthur
28th July: Pleve, Minister of the Interior, is murdered

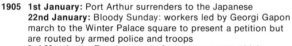

1905 **1st January:** Port Arthur surrenders to the Japanese
22nd January: Bloody Sunday: workers led by Georgi Gapon march to the Winter Palace square to present a petition but are routed by armed police and troops
3rd March: the Tsar issues a reform programme which includes plans for a consultative body, the State Duma
Throughout 1905 there are 'mass political strikes' by workers, students, and teaching staff, spreading to Moscow, the Ukraine, Poland, the Baltic states, Finland, the Caucasus, and many Russian cities. Soldiers mutiny in the garrisons at Vladivostok, Tiflis, Tashkent, and Warsaw.
June: Liberal members of the professions form themselves into the 'Union of Unions' presided over by Pavel Milyukov which is later joined by the newly-formed Peasants' Union
27th June: mutiny on board the battleship *Potemkin* briefly joined by the *St George*
5th September: the Treaty of Portsmouth: Russia cedes Port Arthur and Talienwan to Japan
26th October: the St Petersburg Soviet of Workers' Deputies holds its first meeting and throughout November enjoys a semi-official status
30th October: Nicholas signs the 'October Manifesto', conceding the principle of popular control over his power
18th November: Japan establishes a protectorate over Korea
9th December: Nosar, President of St Petersburg Soviet, arrested
16th December: the whole Soviet is arrested while meeting at the building of the Free Economic Society
30th December: Moscow workers come out on strike; the uprising is quelled by troops assisting Governor-General Dubasov
1906 **5th May:** Count Witte is succeeded by Goremykin as Prime Minister
6th May: the Russian Constitution is promulgated
10th May: the First Duma meets in the Tsar's Winter Palace
21st July: it is dissolved; Stolypin becomes Prime Minister
1907 **19th March–16th June:** the Second Duma meets
14th November: the Third Duma assembles

Top: Rasputin and his puppets, the Tsar and Tsarina (left). Lev Trotsky (centre). Women pulling boats on the Volga (right)
Middle: A revolutionary offers the Tsar the choice of a bomb or a Republican bonnet (left). The battleship Potemkin (right).
Bottom: The Tsar baths in the blood of murdered workers (left). General Trepov (centre). The wreckage of Stolypin's carriage after the first attempt to kill him in 1906 (right)

Index of main people, places and events

Author's suggestions
for further reading

Harcave, Sydney
*First Blood: The Russian
Revolution of 1905*
London Bodley Head 1965
Charques, Richard
The Twilight of Imperial Russia
Phoenix House London 1958
Florinsky, Michael T
*Russia: A History and an
Interpretation*
Macmillan NY 1953
Witte, Count Sergei
Memoirs
Heinemann London 1921
Pares, Sir Bernard
Russia and Reform
Constable London 1907
Trotsky, Lev
*A History of the Russian
Revolution*
Gollancz London 1965
Pokrovsky, MN
A Brief History of Russia
Martin Lawrence 1933
Seton-Watson, Hugh
The Decline of Imperial Russia
Methuen 1952
Schwarz, Solomon M
The Russian Revolution of 1905
University of Chicago 1967

The 'Krasny Arkhiv' (Red
Archives), published in Moscow
after the Revolution of 1917
contains, in Russian, the letters
of Nicholas to the Tsarina, the
memoirs of Kuropatkin, Yermolov,
and others.

David Floyd has since 1952
been special correspondent on
Communist affairs for *The Daily
Telegraph*. He served in the
RAF during the Second World
War and as an interpreter on the
British military mission to the
Soviet Union from 1943 to 1947.
Between 1945 and 1951 he was
in the embassies in Moscow,
Prague, and Belgrade

JM Roberts, General Editor of
the *Macdonald Library of the
20th Century*, is Fellow and Tutor
in Modern History at Merton
College, Oxford. He is also
General Editor of Purnell's
History of the 20th Century
and Joint-Editor of the *English
Historical Review*, and author of
Europe 1880-1945 in the Long-
man's History of Europe. He has
been English Editor of the
*Larousse Encyclopedia of
Modern History*, has reviewed for
The Observer, New Statesman,
and *Spectator*, and given talks on
the BBC

Library of the 20th Century

Publisher: John Selwyn Gummer
Editor: Christopher Falkus
Executive Editor: Jonathan Martin
Editorial Assistant: Jenny Ashby
Designed by: Brian Mayers/
Germano Facetti
Design: Prospective Designs
Research: Jasmine Gale